Companion To The Psalter

A Devotional Guide
To The Psalms

Robert G. Beckstrand

CSS Publishing Company, Inc., Lima, Ohio

COMPANION TO THE PSALTER

Copyright © 2007 by
CSS Publishing Company, Inc.
Lima, Ohio

The original purchaser may photocopy material in this publication for use as it was intended (worship material for worship use; educational material for classroom use; dramatic material for staging or production). No additional permission is required from the publisher for such copying by the original purchaser only. Inquiries should be addressed to: Permissions, CSS Publishing Company, Inc., 517 South Main Street, Lima, Ohio 45804.

Scripture quotations are from the New Revised Standard Version of the Bible, copyright 1989 by the Division of Christian Education of the National Council of the Churches of Christ in the USA. Used by permission.

Library of Congress Cataloging-in-Publication Data

Beckstrand, Robert G., 1925-
  Companion to the Psalter : a devotional guide to the Psalms / Robert G. Beckstrand.
    p. cm.
  Includes index.
  ISBN 0-7880-2464-7 (perfect bound : alk. paper)
 1. Bible. O.T. Psalms—Devotional use. I. Title.

 BS1430.54.B35 2007
 242'.5—dc22

2007023883

For more information about CSS Publishing Company resources, visit our website at www.csspub.com or email us at csr@csspub.com or call (800) 241-4056.

Cover design by Barbara Spencer
ISBN-13: 978-0-7880-2464-1
ISBN-10: 0-7880-2464-7   PRINTED IN USA

To
Dorothy
my loving,
encouraging wife

Table Of Contents

Foreword	7
Suggestions For Using This Handbook	9
Some Key Words In The Psalms	11
Facts About The Five Collections Or Books	13
Psalm Types	15
Life And Death In The Psalms	19
The Poetry Of The Psalms	21
Where To Look In The Psalms	23
Suggestions For Using The Psalms In The Church Year	25
What Some Have Said About The Psalms	29
Book One Psalms 1 through 41	31
Book Two Psalms 42 through 72	103
Book Three Psalms 73 through 89	163
Book Four Psalms 90 through 106	199
Book Five Psalms 107 through 150	235
Psalm Index	327
Lutheran Church Year Psalm Placements	333
Resources	335

Foreword

The psalms were introduced to me in my childhood. My mother would lead our family in the reciting of a favorite psalm each morning at the breakfast table. She had memorized at least ten, and she expected us to learn to recite them with her as best we could. We children soon knew them by memory. She always recited them with an appreciation of their beautiful poetic cadence and with conviction.

During my service in World War II, the turbulent college years that followed, and my more than forty years of ministry, the Holy Spirit recalled portions of these psalms to me and encouraged my faith. A few examples:

> *God is our refuge and strength, a very present help in trouble. Therefore we will not fear....* — Psalm 46:1

> *The LORD shall keep thee from all evil; he shall preserve thy soul.* — Psalm 121:7

> *The LORD is good, his mercies are everlasting, and his truth endureth to all generations.* — Psalm 100:5

I use the psalms as part of each day's devotions, using a Daily Lectionary. Recently I read how the Venerable Bede chanted or recited in the monastery the entire Psalter every two weeks, and made for himself an **"Abbreviated Psalter"** to help him identify and recall each psalm. I made, for my use, my own Abbreviated Psalter, then added the **theme** and **type** for each psalm, some explanatory **notes**, a suggestion for **reflection**, and then a **prayer** relating the theme or the motifs in the psalm to the New Testament faith. Parish members have, at times, expressed to me their perplexity with the psalms and their desire to understand and make use of them. I submit my notes to all who may find them helpful to be used as an introduction and encouragement for the reader's own studies, meditation, discoveries, and inspiration.

I've added simple, short summaries on the following:

- suggestions for using this handbook;
- some key words in the psalms (covenant language);

- facts about the five collections or books;
- psalm types;
- where to look in the psalms;
- suggestions for using the psalms in the church year; and
- what some have said about the psalms.

An Index in chart form lists each psalm with 1) type, 2) author or source, and 3) use in the Revised Common Lectionary. Resources I have enjoyed and used and to which I am indebted are listed after the Index. They should be considered for further studies in the psalms.

I have restricted my use to the New Revised Standard Version for the sake of convenience in memorizing, for its faithfulness to the Hebrew text, and its similarity to the King James Version. I recommend its almost exclusive use to everyone for reading the psalms.

I hope these studies will open up the psalms to many, who want a simple help and guide in using them devotionally. They won't miss out on the blessings the Lord gives in this vital part of his word to us.

— Robert G. Beckstrand

Suggestions For Using This Handbook

Read one or two psalms every day. It is helpful to follow the suggestions of the Sunday lectionary or the daily lectionary throughout the church year. After reading and meditating on the psalm, turn to this companion for further study and reflection.

The prayer for each psalm can be a closing response to one's devotional time. It expresses the psalm's theme or motif and relates it to the entire story of God's revelation and of Christ. Some psalms describe sufferings like Jesus endured; some prophetically express the hope that his kingdom is fulfilled. The psalms will help us better understand our Lord Jesus; they were the hymnal and prayerbook used by him and the early church.

This book will be helpful

- to anyone seeking a brief and easy help toward understanding, reflecting, and appreciating a psalm;
- to all who do not have access to, or time for, consulting commentaries with involved discussion of scholarly issues and original language;
- to people who have been asked to lead the devotions for a meeting;
- to lectors leading the psalm in worship service;
- to people wanting to learn how to pray to God in various situations and moods;
- to students seeking to understand the outlook and piety of Bible personalities; and
- to people wanting to use a psalm in daily devotions, or the daily office.

Through the psalms, the Holy Spirit

- *encourages* us to seek the Lord;
- *gives* to us a richer understanding of God and of Jesus;
- *teaches* us how to pray, to open up to God and express what we are feeling or experiencing;
- *shows* us honesty in prayer (the psalmist says it like it is);
- *provides* examples of ordinary people giving vent to disappointment with God and yet trusting him;

- *leads* us to repentance, and helps us express it;
- *strengthens* us in loyal trust in God, even when we, like the psalmists, may be tried in the fires of doubt;
- *reveals* the reality of exuberant joy in the Lord, that we too may catch it and sound forth our praise;
- *teaches* a panoramic view of history and of God's activity leading to Christ;
- *unites* Christians of all kinds. Luther, Xavier, Wesley, Calvin, Newman, and other Christians of all varieties have used and loved the psalms; and
- *anchors* us in both realism and hope.

In the book of Psalms, the Holy Spirit has provided us a marvelous resource for our use and joyful benefit. We neglect it to our sore loss.

This book has been formatted to allow space for your personal notes in the outside margins.

Some Key Words In The Psalms

1. **Psalm** — song

2. **Covenant** — an agreement between two or more people. God condescended to be a covenanting party, made a free promise on his part, continued life and favor, and asked the fulfillment of certain conditions by man — obedience to his law. (See Exodus 19-24, especially 24:1-8.) Creation and the Covenant are the two basic realities testified to in the Old Testament.

3. **Lord** — when in capital letters, it denotes the Hebrew word **Yahweh** (the sacred name of the covenanting God, meaning "I AM"). Devout Jews would not say the name aloud when the scriptures were read and would substitute for it the word, "Lord." Most translations continue to respect this custom, so that when capitalized, **Lord** means Yahweh, but when in lower case, **Lord** means Master. The other most used Hebrew designation for God is **Elohim**, meaning "the Mighty One," and is translated simply **God**.

4. **Law (Torah)** — the guidance or instruction that comes from God (through priests or prophets). "It is the whole content of God's revelation of his nature and purpose, which incidentally makes clear man's responsibility before God."[1] It also was used to designate the books of Moses, or Pentateuch, and, at times, the commands and directives of God, determined by context. It includes the big story of God's saving acts and electing grace.

5. **Steadfast love** *(chesed)* — God's covenant favor, love, and loyalty to Israel, and what God is doing and will do for Israel (his servant people in the world).

6. **Godly, the upright** *(chasid)* — our part in the covenant, the loyalty God expects of us in response to his grace: faithfulness to him.

7. **Righteousness** — that which conforms to the norm — and the norm is the character of God. It is right action and fair dealing man to man. It also means justice.

8. **God's Name** — his reputation, revealed in his mighty activity for our redemption and his dealings with Israel. Also the memory of his revelation, his mighty acts.

9. **Judge** — God as governor over against man's rebellion, mismanagement, and disorder; his redeeming work of putting down evil and creating good.

10. **Praise** — to exult in, to enjoy, to be happy with, to rejoice in — and saying so to others and to God.

11. **Sheol** — the abode of the dead, "continued existence in the underworld, a region of shadows, misery, and futility."[2]

---

1. Alan Richardson, *A Theological Word Book Of The Bible* (New York: MacMillan, 1950), p. 122.

2. *Ibid*, p. 106.

Facts About The Five Collections Or Books

Book One (Psalms 1-41)
These are the earliest psalms, with individual expression, nearly all by David, reflecting circumstances in his life. There is consistent use of Yahweh (The LORD) for the name of God. The recurring theme is the ultimate prosperity of the righteous and the destruction of the wicked.

Book Two (Psalms 42-72) and Book Three (Psalms 73-89)
"The Elohistic Psalter," using "Elohim" (the Mighty One) for God, is expressed in Book Two. These have various writers: Korahites (42-49), Asaph (50; 73-85; 87-89), David (51-71), and Solomon (72). Book Three shows a national and historical interest, as well as an exaltation of the temple.

Book Four (Psalms 90-106) and Book Five (Psalms 107-150)
These are of comparatively later dates (exile and after). They portray liturgical character used in temple worship with some national and historical emphasis. They include the following groups: Kingship of God (Psalms 93; 95-100), Hallels (Psalms 113-118), Songs of Ascents (Psalms 120-134), and the Hallelujah Psalms (Psalms 145-150).

Note On The Titles
The titles at the head of each psalm are of interest to the historian. There are musical terms or directions, liturgical details, and authorship (many probably indicating merely the source from which they were obtained or derived). **Selah** occurs 71 times in the psalms and is believed to be a musical or liturgical sign of some kind.

Psalm Types

The general characteristics of each psalm is indicated on the first line of each psalm's Notes and in the Index. Some psalms fit in more than one category and are so noted.

1. Hymns of Praise
   General
   Lord of Creation
   Lord of History (including Israel's "holy history")
   Kingship of God (Enthronement) (see B)
   Royal Messianic (see C)
2. Laments — Prayers in times of trouble (see D)
   General
   Messianic Suffering (see E)
   Penitential (see F)
   Imprecatory (see G)
3. Affirmations of Faith
4. Songs of Thanksgiving (Community or Individual)
5. Wisdom Poetry (see H)
6. Liturgies (some Prophetic, some Instructive)
7. Acrostic or Alphabetical (see I)
8. Mixed

A. **Praise** — These are expressions of joy, adoration, deep appreciation, and high regard for God. God is to be loved, trusted, and enjoyed!

B. **Kingship of God/Enthronement Psalms** — (47; 93; 96; 98; 99) These are celebrating God's coming to be judge of all the earth. They have a double meaning: a) relating to circumstances experienced when written, and b) to the future unfolding of God's plan for the world. The nations of the world are spoken of as belonging to God and coming to the time when they all will acknowledge his sovereignty. Israel was God's agent for accomplishing this. "I know that Messiah is coming (who is called Christ). When he comes he will proclaim all things to us" (John 4:25).

C. **Royal Messianic** — (2; 18; 20; 21; 45; 61; 72; 89; 101; 110; 132; 144) Israel's king was an "anointed one" (Messiah). God's purpose in electing Israel as his representative was to establish a universal kingdom on earth. Representing the nation was its king, appointed by God. The promise of sovereignty over all the nations was given to David and his house. These psalms express this expectation in various ways. After the exile, the people turned to look for one who would fulfill all that had been promised to Israel's king.

D. **Laments** — These are expressions of sorrow, a crying out of grief, or a complaint of a deplorable situation.

E. **Messianic Suffering** — (22; 35; 41; 55; 69) Jesus said, "Everything written about me in the law of Moses, the prophets, and the psalms must be fulfilled" (Luke 24:44). These psalms aroused expectations, kept hope alive, and enabled worshipers to realize how through long ages God was preparing for the coming of a special "anointed one" or Messiah. The thought of the righteous suffering for the sake of God's purpose and glory were anticipations of the sufferings of Christ. Some details prefigured the actual Passion of Christ. These psalms can help us understand what our Lord was going through, something of his feelings as he faced his foes and the cross. He prayed these psalms.

F. **Penitentials** — (6; 32; 38; 51; 102; 130; 140) These express repentance for sin, expressions of sorrow, guilt, and regret for one's misdeeds, with desire for forgiveness and restoration, not hopeless remorse or self-hatred.

G. **Imprecatory or Cursing Psalms** — (35; 69; 109) These are shocking, but notice these important facts about them:

1. They are *prayers* and to be understood as prayers,
2. They show *restraint*. The psalmist is not taking revenge. He is asking God to do that. He realizes that revenge was God's responsibility first, and his when God directed.
3. The *enemies* are opposing God's cause in this world and are not merely those of a personal conflict. The *plea* is for

   God, the rightful judge, to put down the wicked behavior and to carry out his desires for justice in this world. If this is God's world, let it be so!
  4. C. S. Lewis says these psalms show what wrongdoing does to its victims: it causes them to hate. (This is the real damage.) The spiritual maturity exemplified by Jesus and his express teaching tell us to pray for our enemies, to do good to those who despise us, and to become like our Father in heaven.

H. **Wisdom** — Along with the law and the prophets, this was one of the departments of knowledge among the Hebrews (Job, Proverbs, Ecclesiastes, and other passages of scripture).

I. **Acrostic or Alphabetical Psalms** — (9; 10; 25; 34; 37; 111; 112; 119; 145) These are where each verse begins with a successive letter of the Hebrew alphabet, probably as an aide for teaching and memorization as well as for meditation.

Life And Death In The Psalms

Death was never regarded as the end of personal existence, but the future was sad. The dead could not enjoy communion with God or experience his steadfast love. While to the persecuted it was regarded as a welcome rest, it was still a monotonous and hopeless gloom. Nowhere is there hope of a resurrection from the dead (Psalms 6:5; 30:9; 88:3-7). An excellent study of this is Part One of *The Resurrection of the Son of God* by N. T. Wright (Minneapolis: Fortress Press, 2003).

A few rare utterances in the psalms however, indicate the faith and hope of an unending fellowship with God. "Unquestionably these psalms (16; 17; 49; 73) do contain the germ and principle of the doctrine of eternal life," according to A. F. Kirkpatrick.[1]

We read these passages in the light of fuller revelation and realize the Holy Spirit inspired their authors to be confident that God did not intend to create fellowship with humans only to let it be suddenly and finally terminated by the bleak and shadowy existence of Sheol. C. S. Lewis spoke of God as a lover who woos instead of ravishes. We could add that he is a lover who doesn't "love 'em and leave 'em," but whose love is, like the given covenant love, steadfast and of undeserved favor, even in death. The full revelation of this could only be given by the actual suffering, death, and resurrection of Jesus Christ. No one would have dared to believe such a prospect had it not happened with Christ.

Why the delay of such great news? Humankind needed the long training to know the sting of death as punishment of sin, to be impressed with the tragedy and lack of fulfillment of life here, and to long for something better. "The faint glimmerings of twilight in the eschatological darkness of the Old Testament are the first rays of the coming sunrise."[2]

The early Hebrews' faith was a stark contrast to that of the Egyptians. God directed the Hebrews to concentrate on responsibilities and possibilities for this life for everyone. The Egyptians spent their energies preparing for a future existence for their royalty.

1. A. F. Kirkpatrick, *The Psalms* (New York: Cambridge University Press, 1957), p. xcv.

2. *Ibid*, p. xcvi.

The Poetry Of The Psalms

The main characteristic of Hebrew poetry is its rhythm. In a rhythmic balance of clauses there is a symmetry of form and sense called *parallelism*. Three kinds of parallelism are:

1. Synonymous parallelism — when the same thought is repeated with different words in the second line of a verse or couplet.
   *"When Israel went out from Egypt,
   The house of Jacob from a people of strange language ..."*
   (Psalm 114:1).
2. Contrasting parallelism — when a thought is explained by its opposite in the second line.
   *"For the LORD watches over the way of the righteous,
   but the way of the wicked will perish"* (Psalm 1:6).
3. Constructive parallelism — when the two lines are synonymous or express cause/consequence, enlarging on the thought.
   *"Though an army encamp against me,
     my heart shall not fear;
   though war rise up against me,
     yet I will be confident"* (Psalm 27:3).

Another feature of Hebrew poetry in the psalms is the use of acrostic or alphabetical order, where each verse begins with a successive letter of the Hebrew alphabet (9; 10; 25; 34; 37; 111; 112; 119; 145). Consult commentaries for further details.

Where To Look In The Psalms

Confession and Forgiveness — 6; 25; 32; 38; 51; 102; 130; 143

Depression — 13; 42; 43; 102; 142; 143

Family — 127; 128

God's Help in Trouble — 13; 31; 46; 55; 57; 69; 77; 107

God's Personal Care — 27; 91; 139

God's Word — 19; 119; 138

Glory of the Creator — 19; 104; 147; 148

Harvest — 65; 67; 145

Israel's Story — 78; 105; 114; 116

Messianic King — 2; 20; 21; 72; 110

Missions — 67; 96; 98; 117

Morning/Evening — 3; 4

National Life — 9; 11; 12; 33; 82; 101; 146

Riches — 49; 73

Sickness — 18; 38
    Recovery — 30; 116
    Old Age — 71
    Death — 16; 39; 73; 116

Suffering Messiah — 13; 17; 22; 31; 35; 41; 55; 56; 69; 86

Thanksgiving and Praise — 8; 34; 40; 84; 95; 96; 98; 100; 103; 138; 145; 146-150

Travel/Moving — 121

Suggestions For Using The Psalms In The Church Year

Psalms Of The Day for each Sunday are listed in order, Year A, Year B, Year C. Other suggested psalms for that season follow.

Advent
    1 — 122; 80; 25
    2 — 72; 85; Luke 1:68-79
    3 — 146; 126; Isaiah 12
    4 — 80; 89; 80
    also 11; 24; 40; 43; 62; 85; 123; 124; 130

Christmas
    Christmas Day — 96; 97; 98
    1 — 148
    2 — 147
    also 20; 89; 102; 112; 113

Epiphany
    The Epiphany Of Our Lord — 72
    The Baptism Of Our Lord (Epiphany 1) — 29
    2 — 40; 139; 36
    3 — 27; 62; 19
    4 — 15; 111; 71
    5 — 112; 147; 138
    6 — 119:1-8; 30; 1
    7 — 119:33-40; 41; 37
    8 — 131; 103; 92
    The Transfiguration Of Our Lord — 2; 50; 99
    also 57; 67; 72; 81; 96; 97; 99

Lent
    Ash Wednesday — 51
    1 — 32; 25; 91
    2 — 121; 22; 27
    3 — 95; 19; 62
    4 — 23; 107; 32
    5 — 130; 51; 126

Passion/Palm Sunday — 31
    also 6; 13; 31; 32; 69; 86; 90; 117; 143

Holy Week
    Monday — 36
    Tuesday — 71
    Wednesday — 70
    Maundy Thursday — 116
    Good Friday — 22

Easter Day — 118

Easter
    2 — 16; 133; 118
    3 — 116; 4; 30
    4 — 23
    5 — 31; 22:25-31; 148
    6 — 66; 98; 67
    Ascension — 47
    7 — 68; 1; 97
    also 33; 98; 105; 117; 136; 139

The Day Of Pentecost — 104:24-34, 35b
    also 30; 103; 104; 139

Holy Trinity — 8; 29; 8

Propers (after Pentecost)
    May 24-28 — 131; 103; 92
    May 29-June 4 — 31; 81; 96
    June 5-11 — 50; 130; 30
    June 12-18 — 100; 92; 32
    June 19-25 — 69; 107; 22
    June 26-July 2 — 89; 30; 16
    July 3-9 — 145; 123; 66
    July 10-16 — 65; 85; 25
    July 17-23 — 86; 23; 15
    July 24-30 — 119:129-136; 145; 138
    July 31-August 6 — 145; 78; 49
    August 7-13 — 85; 34; 33

August 14-20 — 67; 34; 82
August 21-27 — 138; 34; 103
August 28-September 3 — 26; 15; 112
September 4-10 — 119:33-40; 146; 1
September 11-17 — 103; 116; 51
September 18-24 — 145; 54; 113
September 25-October 1 — 25; 19; 146
October 2-8 — 80; 8; 37
October 9-15 — 23; 90; 111
October 16-22 — 96; 91; 121
October 23-29 — 1; 126; 84
October 20-November 5 — 43; 119:1-8; 32
November 6-12 — 70; 146; 17
November 13-19 — 90; 16; 98
Christ The King — 95; 93; 46

Reformation Sunday — 46
All Saints — 34; 24; 149
Thanksgiving Day — 65; 126; 100
Stewardship Of Creation — 104

What Some Have Said About The Psalms

Our Risen Lord Jesus Christ
"These are my words that I spoke to you while I was still with you — that everything written about me in the law of Moses, the prophets, and the psalms must be fulfilled" (Luke 24:44).

Saint Paul
"Be filled with the Spirit, as you sing psalms and hymns and spiritual songs among yourselves, singing and making melody to the Lord in your hearts, giving thanks to God the Father at all times and for everything in the name of our Lord Jesus Christ" (Ephesians 5:18-20).

Saint Augustine
"In what accents I addressed Thee, my God, when I read the Psalms of David, those faithful songs, the language of devotion which banishes the spirit of pride ... How my love for Thee was kindled by them! How I burned to recite them, were it possible, throughout the world, as an antidote to the pride of humanity" (*Confessions* IX, 4).

Martin Luther
"Whenever I feel that I have grown cold and disinclined to pray, because of other tasks and thoughts (for the flesh and the devil always prevent and hinder prayer), I take my little Psalter, hasten into my room, or, if it is during the day and I have time, to the church where others are gathered, and begin to say the Ten Commandments, the Creed, and then, if I have time, some words of Christ, Paul, or the Psalm, saying them quietly to myself just as children do" (*A Simple Way To Pray*, "For Master Peter, the Barber," p. 1).

Philip Yancey
"I come to the psalms not primarily as a student wanting to acquire knowledge, but rather as a fellow pilgrim wanting to acquire relationship. The first and greatest commandment is to love the Lord our God with all our hearts and all our souls and all our minds. More than any other book in the Bible, Psalms reveals what

a heartfelt, soul-starved, single-minded relationship with God looks like ... It contains the anguished journals of people who want to believe in a loving, gracious, faithful God while the world keeps falling apart around them ... The psalms give me a model of spiritual therapy" (*The Bible Jesus Read*, Chapter 4 [New York: Zondervan, 2002]).

Book One
Psalms 1 through 41

1
Happy Are Those ...

Happy are those who do not follow the advice of the wicked,
 or take the path that sinners tread,
 or sit in the seat of scoffers;
*but their delight is in the law of the L*ORD*,*
 and on his law they meditate day and night ...
*The L*ORD *watches over the way of the righteous,*
 but the way of the wicked will perish.
— Psalm 1:1, 2, 6

Theme: The two ways in life

Outline

1-3   Avoiding the principles and practices of those who offend the LORD, the godly seek God's word as their guide of life and are truly blessed.

4-6   The ungodly ("wicked") serve no worthwhile purpose, have no stability and perish.

Notes
- Wisdom Poetry
- This is a teaching psalm, a prologue to the whole Psalter, an invitation to the devout life.
- Key word is law (Torah). It is used to denote:
  a. instruction,
  b. a body of teaching,
  c. laws or code of laws,
  d. the five books of Moses that contain accounts of election, grace, covenant, and redemption as well as laws, and in its widest sense came to be (as here), and
  e. the "word" of the LORD, all divine revelation as the guide of life.

  What the Christian refers to as "the gospel" is anticipated in the Torah.
- "LORD" in capital letters denotes the sacred name of the covenant God, "I AM" (Yahweh), which devout Jews would not utter aloud but spoke for it the word, "Lord," meaning Master

and owner of each member of the human family, claiming full obedience. Most modern translations observe this tradition.

For Reflection
- There are two ways of living. Which shall I consciously take? What kind of self-denial is called for?
- How do I make use of the basic resource and activity of the godly life? (v. 2).
- What is it to "delight in the law of the Lord"?
- What are the streams of water bringing sustenance and fruit? (See John 5:37-39.)

Prayer
Lord God, you invite us into a living fellowship with you through your Word-become-flesh, Jesus Christ, your Son. May this revelation of you protect, nourish, and refresh us and bring forth in life and in death the good fruits of your Spirit, through Jesus Christ our Lord. Amen.

2
Why Do The Nations Conspire And The Peoples Plot In Vain?

"I have set my king on Zion, my holy hill."
  I will tell of the decree of the LORD:
He said to me, "You are my son ...
Ask of me, and I will make the nations your heritage,
  and the ends of the earth your possession."
Happy are all who take refuge in him.
— Psalm 2:6-7b, 8, 11c

Theme: God's promise to his anointed one

Outline
A drama in four acts
1-3   Act 1: The nations are in rebellion against God.
4-6   Act 2: God's judgment and plan for his "anointed."
7-9   Act 3: The anointed (king) trusts God's promise.
10-12 Act 4: This age of grace with a warning to all rulers.

Notes
- Royal Messianic
- The psalm's origin may have been in the early reign of Solomon, when subject nations were threatening revolt. The king as the Lord's anointed was his viceroy and earthly representative, and rebellion against him was rebellion against the Lord.
- It is prophetic of the true conditions of the kingdom of Christ, assaulted by the kingdoms of the world. "This Second Psalm supplied the first prayer and words of thanksgiving to God in the church of the New Testament."[1]
- Zion, poetical and prophetic name for Jerusalem, the earthly dwelling-place of Yahweh and seat of his kingdom. See note for Psalm 48.
- Read Acts 4:23-31 to see how the early church used this psalm.
- "Kiss his feet" = be subject to him. (See Mark 9:7; 1 John 3:23.)

For Reflection
- Where was Jesus in this drama?
- Where are we in the drama?
- How can the message of this psalm encourage us when we are confronted with rejections of our Lord Jesus Christ?

Prayer
Lord God, you gave us your beloved Son to be our king, enthroned on the cross. Give us a humility like his, the joy of his rule of grace, and the faithfulness to bear witness of him to others, in the leading and presence of your Spirit. Amen.

---

1. Martin Luther, *Luther's Works*, Volume 12 (St. Louis: Concordia Publishing House, 1973), p. 5, pp. 3-93. Refers to Acts 4:25-28.

3
How Many Are My Foes?

I cry aloud to the LORD,
and he answers me from his holy hill.
I lie down and sleep;
I wake again, for the LORD sustains me
— Psalm 3:4-5

Theme: Trust in God under adversity

Outline
1-2 David lays out his urgent need to the LORD.
3-4 He remembers God is his protector.
5-6 Amid danger, he trusts God will sustain him.
7-8 He prays for deliverance and blessing for the people.

Notes
- Lament
- A morning psalm, companion to Psalm 4. Verse 5 is a great way to begin every day.
- David may have been fleeing from Absalom. (See 2 Samuel 15-18.)
- Dietrich Bonhoeffer found comfort from this psalm while in prison.

For Reflection
- Many foes trouble God's people (v. 1). One should not confine the psalm's meaning to David's situation. Who are our foes? They also are many:
  a. influences toward unbelief or despair (like v. 2),
  b. our sins and tendencies to sin and hardness of heart,
  c. the cruelties and indifference of others,
  d. the anxiety of death, and
  e. the evil one.

  The psalms were prayed by people in the midst of conflict. The Holy Spirit preserves them for the blessing of all in such struggles, urging us to pray and trust the LORD.

- This despair (v. 2) is a denial of God's grace and goodness, the voice of unbelief, an affront to the character of God. What "shields" us from giving in to it? (See 2 Corinthians 4:6-8.)
- What does it mean to trust the Lord as the one "who lifts up my head" and "sustains me"? (See Nehemiah 9:21 cf; Psalm 55:22; Luke 22:31-32.)
- The "holy hill" refers to Mount Zion, where the temple stood. It was the place where sacrifice was offered, and it symbolized God's presence and revelation. For the Christian, God answers our cries wonderfully from his holy hill (it's called Calvary). (See John 3:16.)

Prayer
Lord God, when his faint-hearted disciples and his foes thought his condition hopeless, your beloved Son, like David, trusted you to lift up his head and sustain him. Remembering your faithfulness to them, give us faith to be confident in you and to rest in your loving care. Amen.

4
Answer Me When I Call

I will both lie down and sleep in peace;
for you alone, O Lord, make me lie down in safety.
— **Psalm 4:8**

Theme: Confident plea for deliverance from enemies

Outline
1 Appeal to God.
2-3 Counsel to the rebels.
4-5 What to do when disturbed: quiet trust in the Lord.
6-8 Gladness and confidence in the Lord.

Notes
- Affirmation of Faith
- An evening prayer (companion to Psalm 3), an antidote to anxiety for the morrow, a reminder of our only real security in the recurring dangers of life.
- It seems to follow the situation of Psalm 3.
- "God of my right!" = my Defender, Vindicator, my Righteousness (v. 1).
- "The faithful" (*chasid*, derived from *chesed*, steadfast love), a term describing the recipient and sharer of the covenant love of God (v. 3).

For Reflection
- Verses 6-8 suggest gladness and peace can be ours even if our outward circumstances are disturbing. Do these gifts come from cultivating optimistic thinking or the knowledge of God? (See Philippians 4:4; 1 Timothy 1:12.)

Prayer
Praise be to you, Lord God, for showing yourself to David and to your beloved Son as one able and willing to sustain them in their distresses. Give to us that quiet trust, that we may both rest and rise in your service now and on our last day. Amen.

5

Give Ear To My Words, O Lord, Give Heed To My Sighing

*O Lord, in the morning you hear my voice;
in the morning I plead my case to you,
and watch.*

— Psalm 5:3

Theme: A morning prayer

Outline
1-3   Lord, listen to my sighs and cries.
4-6   You hate evil — that assures me.
7-8   Because of my enemies, I need your righteous leading.
9-10 My enemies are also your enemies! May they fall!
11-12 May the godly rejoice in your favor and protection.

Notes
- Lament
- "Your name" = a way of referring to the character and attributes God has revealed of himself (and thus his reputation among the faithful).
- Notice a pattern of prayer that is recurrent in the psalms:
   a. the cry of distress or anguish in the struggle with sin and evil;
   b. calmer pleading, reasons for God to respond, recalling God's character, his steadfast love; and
   c. joy and confidence in the decision to trust and hope in the Lord — the Spirit bringing the psalmist around to the simple decision to trust the Lord, from anxiety to hope.

For Reflection
- "In the morning you hear my voice" indicates the wholesome discipline of praying at the beginning of the day, a "quiet time with God" (v. 3). One woman said, "My first duty each day is to let myself be happy in the Lord." Was this not the attitude of the psalmist (v. 7) in all his worship? If we practice such a discipline, what will we subconsciously "watch" for the rest of the day?

Prayer
Lord God, you hate the refusal of your call to a covenant walk with you. Lead us in the ways of your righteousness, justice, and love, so that, with the whole church, we, and all who seek you, may rejoice together in your Son, Jesus Christ our Lord. Amen.

6
Do Not Rebuke Me In Your Anger

Be gracious to me, O LORD,
for I am languishing;
O LORD, heal me, for my bones
are shaking with terror ...
Turn, O LORD, save my life;
deliver me for the sake of your steadfast love.
— **Psalm 6:2, 4**

Theme: Prayer for recovery from grave illness

Outline
1-3   Cry for healing of body and mind.
4-7   Continued pleading with an attempt to reason with God.
8-10 Joy and confidence return.

Notes
- Lament — Penitential
- The first of seven Penitential Psalms (6; 32; 38; 51; 102; 130; 143).
- Severe illness is the occasion, giving pleasure to evil enemies.
- The plea is based on God's grace, his steadfast love.
- Sheol, the abode of the dead, was regarded with dismay by both Israel and all the ancient world, a diminished shadowy existence, cut off from joy, something to be dreaded. Note similar references in 30:9; 88:10-12; 115:17; and also Hebrews 2:15. (See the note on "Life And Death In The Psalms" in the introductory pages.)

For Reflection
- Is sickness to be thought of as punishment? Some suffering comes from our sin, but Jesus sets limits on that outlook and suggests a different way of regarding it. (See John 9:1-3; Psalm 103:3.)

Prayer
Lord God, you have seen what sin has done to us all, bringing in its wake sickness, suffering, and death. But you have won for us the victory bringing us new life. Restore us to health, that we may live to enjoy and serve you, through Jesus Christ our Lord. Amen.

7
O Lord My God, In You I Take Refuge

O Lord, my God, in you I take refuge;
  save me from all my pursuers, and deliver me ...
O let the evil of the wicked come to an end,
  but establish the righteous,
you who test the minds and hearts,
  O righteous God.
                                           — **Psalm 7:1, 9**

Theme: Appeal to the righteous judge

Outline
1-8   Appeal to God for judgment.
      1-2   I cry for help.
      3-5   I am in the wrong, let the enemy have his way!
      6-8   If you judge me, I am confident!
9-16   Reflections on the fate of the wicked.
      9-10 Bring an end to evil and establish the righteous.
      11-13 You are a righteous judge.
      14-16 Punishment of the wicked comes about by their own actions.
17   Closing thanks and praise.

Notes
- Lament
- The psalm reflects the early years of David as he was hunted by Saul. (See 1 Samuel 14-23.)
- "According to my righteousness" in David's case means, "my innocence of those false accusations — not moral perfection" (v. 8).
- The Lord is active as Judge: testing minds and hearts (v. 9), indignant of those who refuse to repent (vv. 11-13), lets their own misdeeds fall back on themselves (v. 15), bringing an end to evil (v. 9), saving the "upright in heart" (v. 10).

Prayer
O God, you act to bring justice to the world. Give us repentant and upright hearts and minds, cleanse us of sin, and make us a people ever thanking and praising you through Jesus Christ our Lord. Amen.

8
O Lord, Our Sovereign, How Majestic Is Your Name

O Lord, our Sovereign,
  how majestic is your name in all the earth! ...
When I look at your heavens, the work of your fingers,
  the moon and the stars that you have established;
what are human beings that you are mindful of them,
  mortals that you care for them?
                                              — **Psalm 8:1, 3-4**

Theme: Divine majesty and human dignity

Outline
1-2   The revelation of Yahweh's majesty on earth.
3-4   The vastness of the heavens make man seem puny.
5-6   But man is more wonderful than all nature.
7-8   A human is your representative on earth.
9   Chorus (v. 1).

Notes
- Praise — Creation
- "Your name" = your reputation, from the works of creation and providence.

For Reflection
- Jesus quotes verse 2 in reply to the Pharisees at his triumphal entry. (See Matthew 21:16.)
- "Jehovah has ordained that even the feeblest representatives of humanity should be his champions to confound and silence those who oppose his kingdom and deny his goodness ... The mystery of man of a being made in the image of God, is greater than the mystery of the heavens, with all their immensity and majesty ... Man, therefore, even in the weakness of childhood, is a witness of the existence and character of God."[1]
- See how Saint Paul in 1 Corinthians 15:27 and the writer of the letter to the Hebrews (2:6 ff) apply the psalm to the supremacy of Christ.

Prayer

Lord God, our creator, you created us for great things, and you crown us with glory and honor in the gift of your Son, Jesus Christ. By his Spirit within may we be led to praise you with good stewardship of the earth, showing care for the redemption of all that you have made. In the name of Jesus Christ our Lord.

---

1. A. F. Kirkpatrick, *The Psalms* (New York: Cambridge University Press, 1957), p. 38.

9
I Will Give Thanks To The LORD

I will give thanks to the LORD with my whole heart;
I will tell of all your wonderful deeds.
I will be glad and exult in you ...
For you have maintained my just cause ...
Rise up, O LORD! Do not let mortals prevail ...
Put them in fear, O LORD;
let the nations know that they are only human.
— **Psalm 9:1-2a, 4a, 19a, 20**

Theme: Praise God who judges the world with righteousness

Outline
1-4	Praise God for victory!
5-6	The enemies have vanished.
7-10	The LORD judges rightly.
11-12	Sing his praise.
13-14	Prayer for relief.
15-16	The wicked are snared in their own works.
17-18	This gives hope for the future.
19-20	Keep it up, LORD!

Notes
- Acrostic or Alphabetical
- Has pairs of verses beginning with successive letters of the Hebrew alphabet.
- It celebrates the victories of David. It also fits well to apply to the victory of the risen Christ.
- Verses 7-8 portray the judgment of God as ultimate over all nations and ultimately victorious.

For Reflection
- Compare its message with that of the Beatitudes. (See Matthew 5:3-11.)
- What makes verses 15-20 an applicable prayer for our time?

Prayer
Lord God, you judge the world with righteousness. Rescue the afflicted and oppressed. Let all the nations revere you, so that they, with all who seek you, may praise and thank you, through Jesus Christ our Lord. Amen.

10
Why, O LORD, Do You Stand Far Off?

Rise up, O LORD; O God, lift up your hand;
do not forget the oppressed.
Why do the wicked renounce God
and say in their hearts,
"You will not call us to account"? ...
Break the arm of the wicked and evildoers ...
— **Psalm 10:12-13, 15**

Theme: God sees the arrogance and oppression by the wicked

Outline
- 1-2 Complaint: God seems to neglect his people!
- 3-11 The ruthless character and conduct of the wicked.
- 12-13 Plea for the LORD to show his character and intervene.
- 14 The LORD does see our woes, and we can entrust ourselves to his care.
- 15-18 Confident that the LORD will bring justice.

Notes
- Acrostic
- A continuation of Psalm 9.
- Jerome's Vulgate translation considers this part of Psalm 9, as it continues in part with its alphabetical arrangement. (From this point on Roman Catholic versions number one less than Protestant versions.)
- Psalm 9 was a thanksgiving; Psalm 10 is a lament, pleading with God to show himself as the defender of the helpless.

For Reflection
- Verses 3-11 describe the attitude and actions of the wicked.
- Who are the helpless that God is concerned for (described in six ways)? How do we share God's concern for them?
- Seeing how the wicked seem to get away with their unjust dealings and their contempt for God, what hope or comfort does the psalmist find? What place does prayer have in sustaining our faith and hope in the face of evil? Will prayerlessness lead us to acquiesce to evil?

Prayer
O God, you see the arrogance and cruelty of the wicked, the injustices suffered by the oppressed, and you do not forget your people. Give us hope and comfort in our troubles, so that, committing our lives to you, we may with strengthened hearts proclaim your love through Jesus Christ our Lord. Amen.

11
In The Lord I Take Refuge

... how can you say to me,
"Flee like a bird to the mountains"? ...
If the foundations are destroyed,
what can the righteous do? ...
The Lord tests the righteous and the wicked.
— **Psalm 11:1, 3, 5**

Theme: Faith gives courage in faint-heartedness

Outline

1-3	Faint-hearted friends suggest: "You are fighting for a lost cause!"
4-6	The ground of confidence: faith in the Lord.
7	The outlook of faith: "the upright shall behold his face."

Notes
- Affirmation of Faith
- When friends urged David to flee from Saul's growing jealousy, David chose to face danger and duty with trust in God to protect him. (See 1 Samuel 18-21.)

For Reflection
- A valid question for desperate times when injustice and wickedness are rampant and everything is coming loose (v. 3). Why didn't David flee? (See Psalm 16:8 and Hebrews 11:27.)
- There is a time to stay and a time to flee. (See John 10:39-40; Acts 9:24-26; Matthew 10:23; also Genesis 19.)
- Verse 7 is one of the "golden sayings" of the psalter, "fulfilled" in the revelation of the gospel. (See Matthew 5:8.) The source of this confidence is the revealed character and power of God.

Prayer
Lord God, when foundations are shaking and there is no escape, make us mindful of our Lord's trial and victory for us, that we may know our security is in him. Give us courage and love to do that which is right and good in his sight, through Jesus Christ our Lord. Amen.

12
Help, O LORD, For There Is No Longer Anyone Who Is Godly

You, O LORD, will protect us;
 you will guard us from this generation forever.
On every side the wicked prowl,
 as vileness is exalted among humankind.
— Psalm 12:7, 8

Theme: Plea for help in evil times

Outline
1-2   Prayer for help amid prevailing faithlessness.
3-4   For God to silence the insolent.
5-6   God's precious promise of help.
7-8   Confidence in the LORD's protection.

Notes
- Liturgy
- A good prayer for chaotic times of moral and spiritual corruption.
- "The poor" (v. 5) = the powerless, the vulnerable, the humble who have not let wealth, position, or place make them arrogant. (See Matthew 5:3; Luke 6:20.)

For Reflection
- How is the smooth talk of people and the word of God contrasted? How is the truth to be discerned? (See John 8:32; 14:6; and Romans 1:25.)
- Are there others in scripture who felt "I, only I, am left"?

Prayer
When vileness is exalted with smooth talk, protect us by your word, that however powerless and poor in the eyes of others, we may remember your life-giving promises to us of boundless riches in Jesus Christ our Lord. Amen.

13
How Long, O Lord?

How long must I bear pain in my soul,
and have sorrow in my heart all day long?
How long shall my enemy be exalted over me? ...
But I trusted in your steadfast love;
my heart shall rejoice in your salvation.
— **Psalm 13:2, 5**

Theme: A good prayer when depressed

Outline
1-2   Feeling deserted by God's delays,
3-4   he prays for light in the darkness of his despair,
5-6   and resolves to trust, to hope, and to rejoice in the Lord's love.

Notes
- Lament — Penitential (See Psalm 6.)
- The "enemy" — the devil who takes many forms (Luther).
- Steadfast love (*hesed*) — the greatest of all realities. "It ... signifies that continued forbearance of God by which he 'keepeth covenant' (Deuteronomy 7:9) with Israel, even when Israel is slow to keep his commandments and is wayward ... "[1] "The word ... is used in various forms to designate God's dealings with man, and also to indicate the mode in which men ought to deal with one another." The KJV translated the word "mercy" and its faithful recipients, "merciful."[2]
- "How long?" is spoken four times — the eternal human cry.

For Reflection
- When God delays in coming to help us, what are we to do? (See Luke 18:1 ff.)
- See Psalm 130 ("For Reflection").
- Did Jesus pray this prayer with us and for us in his passion?

Prayer
Lord God, the evil one would make us feel deserted and rejected. Your Son overcame him by his death and resurrection, so even as we live in the shadow of death, his victory is promised to us. May the light of your presence shine that we may have hope and joy even in the darkness, through Jesus Christ, your Son our Lord. Amen.

---

1. A. Richardson, *A Theological Wordbook* (New York: MacMillan, 1950), p. 143.

2. R. B. Girdlestone, *Synonymns Of The Old Testament* (Peabody, Massachusetts: Hendrickson Publishers, 2000), p. 111.

14
Fools Say .... There Is No God

Fools say in their hearts, "There is no God."
  They are corrupt, they do abominable deeds;
    there is no one who does good ...
There they shall be in great terror,
  for God is with the company of the righteous.
                    — Psalm 14:1, 5

Theme: Denunciation of godlessness

Outline

1-3 Corruption of humankind comes from failure to seek God.
4-6 Illustrated by their oppression of God's people.
7   A prayer for the day when he brings gladness with deliverance for Israel.

Notes
- Liturgy — Prophetic
- This psalm recurs in Book Two as Psalm 53, with the name Elohim substituted for Yahweh (LORD), and some minor variations. (This is one of a number of indications that the book of Psalms as we have it is a collection from several sources.)
- Verses 1-3 are quoted by Saint Paul (Romans 3:10-12) as one proof among others of the universal corruption of humankind. (See Romans 1:18-21 for the interpretation of vv. 1-3.)

For Reflection
- Atheism is of various kinds. In this psalm it stands for a class of people who are morally perverse and who feel they can succeed as such without interference from God (who they believe has little or no interest or control in human affairs). Hence, they feel free to be cruel when it suits them.

Prayer
Without you, Lord God, all kinds of evil thrive and grow. Let your word shine in our hearts, that we may seek your will and purpose above all and proclaim to the world your grace and power in Jesus Christ our Lord. Amen.

15
O Lord, Who May Abide In Your Tent?

*Those who walk blamelessly and do what is right
and speak the truth from their heart.*
— **Psalm 15:2**

Theme: Who is worthy to dwell in Zion — near the LORD?

Outline
1   The question, "Who is worthy?"
2   The person of integrity, justice, truthfulness.
3-5   Instances of these qualities.
6   Promise of blessing.

Notes
- Liturgy — Instruction
- Probably composed for the bringing of the Ark of the Covenant into the tent, David prepared for it in Zion. (See 2 Samuel 6:17.)
- Probably used by pilgrims with the question of verse 1 answered by the priest (vv. 2-5).

For Reflection
- The condition for an Israelite to have fellowship with God is fulfilling his duty to the neighbor!
- Taking it clause by clause, how does one fare in this self-examination? (See Hebrews 10:19-22.)
- For worthiness to dwell in the presence of God see Psalm 51:11 and Jude 1:24.

Prayer
Lord God, because of our sinfulness we are unfit to live with you. You humbled yourself in Jesus Christ, your Son, to come and dwell with us. We praise you for bringing us to yourself, forgiven and cleansed, and with the promise that we shall dwell one day with you face to face. May we reflect your humility and love to others. Blessed be God: Father, Son, and Holy Spirit. Blessed be God forever. Amen.

16
Protect Me, O God

I keep the LORD always before me;
because he is at my right hand, I shall not be moved.
Therefore my heart is glad, and my soul rejoices,
my body also rests secure.
For you do not give me up to Sheol ...
You show me the path of life.
In your presence there is fullness of joy;
in your right hand are pleasures forevermore.
— **Psalm 16:8-10a, 11**

Theme: Intimations of immortality

Outline
1-4 The marks of the believer: God is the source of his well-being.
5-8 The privilege of the believer: the LORD is his fulfillment and inheritance.
9-11 The future of the believer: life in wonderful fellowship with the LORD.

Notes
- Affirmation of Faith
- Surely this psalm was among the psalms interpreted to the church by the risen Christ. (See Luke 24:25-27, 44, 45.)
- The promise of Christ's resurrection was seen in this psalm by Peter in his sermon at Pentecost (Acts 2:25-33) and by Paul in his sermon at Antioch (Acts 13:35).
- Covenant loyalty (*chasid*) involves not joining in heathen worship (v. 4).

For Reflection
- This is one of four psalms (16; 17; 49; 73) that "contain the germ and principle of the doctrine of eternal life. It was present in the mind of the Spirit who inspired the authors. The intimate fellowship with God, which they speak of as man's highest good and truest happiness, could not, in view of the nature

and destiny of man and his relation to God, continue to be regarded as limited to this life and liable to sudden and final interruption."[1]
- Verses 8-10 are one of the most precious passages in all of scripture. They were certainly dear to Jesus facing the cross, as they are to the Christian facing death and "the things God has in store for us." (See 1 Corinthians 2:9.) They should be memorized, recited each Saturday, the day Jesus' body lay in the tomb. "He who raised up the Lord Jesus will also raise us up with Jesus."
- The psalmist cites at least eight great attributes of God (my refuge, sovereign [Lord], and so on).

Prayer
To know and trust you, Lord, is our greatest privilege and joy in life. Never let it come to an end! Through your beloved Son, who died for us and whom you raised and exalted, bring us to the fulfillment of your loving purpose — life eternal with you. Amen.

---

1. A. F. Kirkpatrick, *The Psalms* (New York: Cambridge University Press, 1957), pp. xcv-xcvi.

17
Hear A Just Cause, O Lord

Wondrously show your steadfast love,
  O Savior of those who seek refuge
  from their adversaries ...
Guard me as the apple of the eye;
  hide me in the shadow of your wings ...
  when I awake I shall be satisfied
    beholding your likeness.
— **Psalm 17:7, 8, 15b**

Theme: Appeal for justice and protection amid enemies

Outline
1-5 Lord, give me justice because of my integrity.
6-12 Protect me — See my enemies, their character, aims, and outlook!
13-14 Overthrow them!
15 What I really want is your fellowship (your "face," "likeness").

Notes
- Lament
- "A just cause" — his appeal is based on his claim of integrity of godly purpose (not sinless innocence). See 1 John 3:21-22 for a similar appeal.

For Reflection
- What kept David from being corrupted by his evil environment?
- Verse 15 is a beautiful expression of Christian hope. Its meaning is unfolded in passages such as John 14:9; 2 Corinthians 3:18; 1 John 3:2; and Revelation 22:4.

Prayer
Lord God, you upheld your Son when he was surrounded by foes. Protect us as the apple of the eye. Hold us to your promises and your paths until we behold you face to face through Jesus Christ our Lord. Amen.

18
I Love You, O Lord

In my distress I called upon the Lord;
to my God I cried for help ...
He reached down from on high, he took me;
he drew me out of mighty waters ...
This God — his way is perfect;
the promise of the Lord proves true;
he is a shield for all who take refuge in him.
— **Psalm 18:6, 16, 30**

Theme: David's personal testimony to God's power and goodness

Outline
1-3   David's experience with God introduced.
4-6   Extreme needs where God rescued him.
7-15 God shows his power in natural phenomena.
16-19 Deliverance was his purpose.
20-24 David's sincere devotion to God.
25-30 God's dealings confirm David's experience.
31-38 David owes all to God's unique character.
39-45 God gave him victory.
46-50 Thanks and praise to him.

Notes
- Royal Messianic
- This psalm, David's thanksgiving, is identical to 2 Samuel 22 with minor variations.
- Probably composed by David in his prime, when struggles with Saul and with the surrounding nations were past, and he was accepted as king by a united people. Nathan had prophesied a great future for his posterity.
- The rulers to come from his line were like him, "anointed ones" (messiahs). From their line the Messiah of messiahs will come and call all people to his kingdom.
- In Romans 15:9 Paul quotes verse 49, applying it as a prophetic anticipation of Christ's final triumph and reign.

For Reflection
- The psalm reflects David's places of refuge in hiding from Saul and in wars with surrounding nations. The rocks and such were tools of God's active protection, but God was not confined to them. Is God's protection dependent on or confined to the defenses and securities we trust in today?

Prayer
Lord God, our strength and salvation in dangers, our light in darkness, give us such strong faith in your way and your promise that we may overcome strife with love, following the example of the promised Messiah, Jesus Christ our Lord. Amen.

19
The Heavens Are Telling
The Glory Of God

The heavens are telling the glory of God;
and the firmament proclaims his handiwork ...
*The law of the L*ORD *is perfect,*
reviving the soul ...
Let the words of my mouth and the meditation of my heart
be acceptable to you,
*O L*ORD*, my rock and my redeemer.*
— **Psalm 19:1, 7a, 14**

Theme: God's glory to be seen in creation and his word (general and special revelation)

Outline

1-6 The universal revelation of God in nature.
7-11 More wonderful is the revelation of his will in his word with its blessings of grace.
12-14 Preserve me and guide me, LORD.

Notes
- Creation and God's word
- "I take this to be the greatest poem in the Psalter and one of the greatest lyrics in the world."[1]
- Verses 7-11 are descriptions of God's word. The Hebrew word for law is Torah, the Covenant charter of Israel (the Five Books of Moses) containing stories of grace, election, and covenant promises as well as laws for the covenant community. Creation and Covenant are the two major themes, the heart of Hebrew faith.
- "Torah does in human life what the sun does within creation: it brings light, power and the searching, probing heat of Yahweh's presence into the depths of the human heart."[2]
- The laws of sacrifice provided atonement for "hidden faults" — those we are unaware of yet (vv. 12-13). For sins committed with proud defiance there was no atonement.

For Reflection
- The sun was worshiped by the Egyptians. Israel saw it as created by God, whose magnificent creative power is a joy to behold.
- List the things God's word, both law and gospel, can do for a person (vv. 7-13).

Prayer
We praise you, O God. The whole creation, so filled with beauty, reflects your glory. May your Spirit and your word accomplish great beauty in our hearts and lives and relationships, so that we may share your saving love and serve you with gladness through our Lord Jesus Christ. Amen.

---

1. C. S. Lewis, *Reflections On The Psalms* (New York: Harcourt, Brace, and World, 1958), p. 63.

2. N. T. Wright, *Paul: In Fresh Perspective* (Minneapolis: Fortress Press, 2005), p. 21.

20
The Lord Answers You In The Day Of Trouble

Now I know that the Lord will help his anointed;
he will answer him from his holy heaven
with mighty victories by his right hand ...
Some take pride in chariots, and some in horses,
but our pride is in the name of the Lord our God.
— **Psalm 20:6, 7**

Theme: A prayer for victory for the king

Outline
1-5 Prayer for the king.
6-8 Anticipation of victory.
9   Prayer for victory.

Notes
- Royal Messianic
- A battle is about to take place. Before a war against foes, both king and people commit their cause to the Lord. Psalm 21 follows after the battle.
- Liturgical psalm: verses 1-5 sung by the congregation, verses 6-8 by priest or prophet or king, verse 9 a concluding prayer by the congregation.

For Reflection
- "Some take pride in chariots...." But what do we trust for our national security today? Weapons? Power? Money? And what for our personal security? (See Luke 19:42 — Jesus' lament over Jerusalem.)

Prayer
Lord God, your Son was victorious over all the powers of evil against us. As we share his conflict and troubles, enable us by your Spirit to be faithful, trusting and obeying you above all other loyalties. Bring us to share in his victory and his eternal life with you. Blessed be God, Father, Son, and Holy Spirit forever. Amen.

21
In Your Strength The King Rejoices

You have given him his heart's desire ...
He asked you for life; you gave it to him —
length of days forever and ever ...
splendor and majesty you bestow on him.
You bestow on him blessings forever;
you make him glad with the joy of your presence.
— Psalm 21:2a, 4, 5b, 6

Theme: Thanksgiving for victory

Outline
Liturgy
1-7   Thanks to God for victory for the king (by congregation or Levites?).
8-12 To the king, future triumphs anticipated (by the priest?).
13   Concluding praise to God from the congregation.

Notes
- Royal Messianic
- This psalm follows Psalm 20, with thanks for victory following the battle.
- "Language which startles us by its boldness ... was adopted and adapted by the Holy Spirit with a prophetic purpose, and only receives its 'fulfillment' in Christ."[1]

For Reflection
- What is the secret of the king's joy?

Prayer
All praise to you, O God, for you exalted Jesus and gave him glory. We praise you for giving us rich blessings and royal dignity through Jesus Christ our Lord. Amen.

---

1. A. F. Kirkpatrick, *The Psalms* (New York: Cambridge University Press, 1957), p. 110.

22
My God, My God, Why Have You Forsaken Me?

Why are you so far from helping me,
*   from the words of my groaning? ...*
All who see me mock at me ...
I am poured out like water ...
*   you lay me in the dust of death ...*
All the ends of the earth shall remember
*   and turn to the L*ORD *...*
*   future generations will be told about the Lord,*
and proclaim his deliverance to a people yet unborn.
      — **Psalm 22:1b, 7a, 14a, 15b, 27a, 30b-31a**

Theme: The crucifixion psalm

Outline

1-21a   My God, my God, *why*?
- 1-2   Cry of agony.
- 3-5   Recalls God's past goodness.
- 6-8   Feels insignificant, is scorned.
- 9-11   Recalls God's past goodness.
- 12-13 Enemies described.
- 14-15 Symptoms of approaching death.
- 16-18 Enemies gloat.
- 19-21 A prayer for God to save him.

21b-31 Praise God!
- 21b-24 He rescued me. Join me in praising him.
- 25-26 He gives renewed zeal for the covenant's purpose.
- 27-28 Looking forward to the LORD's coming reign and rule over all people.
- 29-31 Even the dead shall worship him!

Notes
- Messianic Suffering
- Passion Psalms: 13; 17; 22; 31; 35; 41; 55; 56; 69; 86
- Interpretations:
    a. This is a record of personal experience (David's?).
    b. It is the ideal or typical righteous sufferer.
    c. Israel as a nation is here personified.

d. A prophetic prediction of Christ's passion. "Each of these lines of interpretation contains some truth; none is complete by itself."[1]
- Notice there is no confession of sin, and there are no imprecations.
- The opening words were uttered by Christ on the cross, indicating this psalm was on his mind during the hours of agony. *Eli* (my God) is Hebrew, *Eloi* is Aramaic, the dialect that Jesus spoke. (See Matthew 27:46 and Mark 15:34.)
- From Matthew 27; Mark 15; and Luke 23 see the parallel details with the psalm.

For Reflection
- What are the joyful results of the suffering as described in verses 22-31?
- "The song of praise, begun by the psalmist (v. 22), is taken up by Israel; all the nations of the earth swell the chorus; and the strain echoes on through all the ages. So gloriously ends the psalm that began in the darkest sorrow. *Per crucem ad lucem.* It is a parable of the history of the individual, of Israel, of the Church, of the world."[2]
- When we sound out our "why?" to God, he breaks his silence by the gift of Jesus and the good news of his death and resurrection for us.
- When we experience wrongs done to us, shall we choose to resemble Christ, seeking not revenge but redemption for the enemy? What will we lose doing so?

Prayer
When he hung upon the cross, your Son felt forsaken by all, even by you, and cried, "Why?" You hear the cries of all who feel deserted. You opened the way from death to life for us all in his self-giving unto death. May your people, participating in Christ's sufferings, share blessings and the hope of the gospel with those suffering hunger, weakness, and abandonment. Amen.

---

1. A. F. Kirkpatrick, *The Psalms* (New York: Cambridge University Press, 1957), p. 114.

2. *Ibid*, p. 124.

23
The Lord Is My Shepherd

The Lord is my Shepherd, I shall not want ...
Surely goodness and mercy shall follow me
   all the days of my life.

— Psalm 23:1, 6

Theme: Meditation on the covenant love and providence of God

Outline
1-3   The shepherd provides, renews, and guides.
4   His presence in the darkest time protects and comforts.
5-6   The Lord is a lavish host through eternity.

Notes
- Affirmation of Faith
- The most loved psalm by young and old, Jew and Christian, and wistful agnostic.
- David's early life as shepherd is reflected throughout. Its emphasis is on God's care for the individual.
- "House of the Lord" (v. 6) is wherever God lives — "O God, our help in ages past, our hope for years to come, our shelter from the stormy blast, and our eternal home."[1]

For Reflection
- If I receive all the good shepherd knows that I need (but not everything I may want), what, according to the psalm, will that provide? Verse by verse, list the provisions the shepherd gives each sheep.
- When one looks over one's past and sees times of waywardness, deeds, and attitudes to regret, failures to obey, is it not good to know that his "goodness and mercy shall follow me (to cleanse and renew?) all the days of my life"? What does that do for you?
- "For his name's sake" (v. 3) — not because we deserve it but because God is true to his character; God is faithful. Everything good depends on that.

Prayer
Lord God, how good it is to live by faith under your grace and leading. You tell us we are each dear to you. Through your Son and your Spirit you become ever more near and dear to us. Keep us close to you in faith, leading us through dark valleys that may be ahead, to the heavenly banquet, life eternal through Jesus Christ our Lord. Amen.

---

1. "O God, Our Help In Ages Past," words by Isaac Watts, 1719.

24
The Earth Is The Lord's

The earth is the Lord's and all that is in it,
the world, and those who live in it ...
Lift up your heads, O gates!
and be lifted up, O ancient doors!
that the King of glory may come in.
— Psalm 24:1, 7

Theme: Celebrating the presence of the Lord

Outline
1-2   The Lord of all the earth approaches!
3-6   The moral condition required for access to his presence.
7-10 Procession reaches the gates, which are summoned to open wide to admit their true king.

Notes
- Liturgy — Instruction
- The occasion was the bringing of the ark to Jerusalem (2 Samuel 6). Later addition and use indicates the presence of the temple and its "ancient doors."
- Verses 1-2 were sung as worshipers approached the hill of Zion. At the foot of the hill, a liturgical instruction by the priests (vv. 3-6) was followed when the procession reached the temple gates (vv. 7-10). The choir addressed the gates, "Be lifted up," to receive the representation of the Lord's presence (Ark). Antiphonal song dramatized the climax — the gates are opened and the procession enters.
- This psalm was recited the first day of the week at the morning sacrifice (second temple).

For Reflection
- What does God want in the hearts, souls, hands, and lips in those who worship him?

Prayer

O Lord, how shall I meet you, how welcome you aright?
Your people long to greet you, my hope, my heart's delight!
O kindle, Lord, most holy, your lamp within my breast,
To do in spirit lowly all that may please you best.

Love caused your incarnation; love brought you down to me.
Your thirst for my salvation procured my liberty.
O love beyond all telling, that led you to embrace
In love all love excelling, our lost and fallen race.
— **Paul Gerhardt, 1607-1676**

25
To You, O Lord, I Lift Up My Soul

Make me to know your ways, O Lord;
*   teach my your paths.*
Lead me in your truth, and teach me,
*   for you are the God of my salvation;*
*   for you I wait all day long ...*
My eyes are ever toward the Lord,
*   for he will pluck my feet out of the net.*
— Psalm 25:4-5, 15

Theme: Prayer and reflection on the character of God

Outline
1-7   Prayer for protection, guidance, and forgiveness.
8-15   Reflections on the character and ways of God.
16-21 Concluding prayer for deliverance and preservation.
22   An added prayer for the nation.

Notes
- Alphabetical — Meditation
- Sins = "to miss the mark," denoting the failures, errors, and lapses through the offences of youth (v. 7).
- Transgressions = "rebellions," the deliberate offences perhaps of mature years.

For Reflection
- Almost every verse is a memory gem on which to meditate.
- "Make me to know your ways." What are these ways of God, as cited in verses 8-15? How does Jesus provide the complete and perfect answer to this prayer? What does God do for sinners, for the humble, for those who "fear" him? What effect should this have on one's attitude and actions?

Prayer
O God, our truest, dearest friend, we look to you with trust and hope in your teaching and leading, that all the way through this life we may be faithful followers of your Son and our Savior, the Lord Jesus Christ. Amen.

26
Vindicate Me, O LORD

Vindicate me, O LORD,
  for I have walked in my integrity,
  and I have trusted in the LORD without wavering.
Prove me, O LORD, and try me,
  test my heart and mind.
For your steadfast love is before my eyes,
  and I walk in faithfulness to you.
— Psalm 26:1-3

Theme: A pledge of, and a plea for, loyalty

Outline
1-3 He pleads for God to give recognition to his integrity and single-hearted devotion.
4-8 Evidence of this is in his past conduct and his present joy in worship.
9-10 He pleads to be spared the fate of those who do evil.
11-12 He prays for God to continue to redeem him.

Notes
- Lament
- Verse 3 should read "I walk in *your* faithfulness (or truth), poetically echoing "your steadfast love is before my eyes."
- "Go around your altar" (v. 6) = taking his place in the ring of worshipers around the altar.
- "House in which you dwell" (v. 8) = the tabernacle; the Ark of the Covenant was a symbol of the Presence of God. (See 1 Samuel 4:21-22.)

For Reflection
- Luther said this psalm shows us "how we should behave in relation to the false teachers ... (who) do not even notice or hear the clear, bright, and obvious testimonies of Holy Scripture ...Therefore we should speak just as the prophet David speaks here. He puts into our mouths the words we ought to pray against the false teachers. Would to God that we prayed them!"[1]

- Luther: "The doctrine is pure ... At the same time I still continue to feel the way and nature of the flesh ... especially the subtle poison of ambition ... the mother of all heresies."[2]
- Verse 2 is a brave request to make of God. A similar but more complete one is Psalm 139:24. The Holy Spirit is glad to fulfill that kind of request. Will the result or effect be humbling? Or encouraging? Or both?

Prayer
Lord Jesus, you are the example of true faithfulness and integrity. You reveal the glory of the Father to us. May your holiness keep before us your undeserved and steadfast love and enable us to walk faithfully in your truth. Amen.

---

1. Martin Luther, *Luther's Works*, Volume 12 (St. Louis: Concordia Publishing House, 1973), p. 184 ff.

2. *Ibid.*

27
The Lord Is My Light And My Salvation

One thing I asked of the Lord,
that will I seek after:
to live in the house of the Lord
all the days of my life,
to behold the beauty of the Lord,
and to inquire in his temple.
Wait for the Lord;
be strong, and let your heart take courage;
wait for the Lord!
— **Psalm 27:4, 14**

Theme: There's no need to fear, but I still do!

Outline
1-6 I am confident and joyful in the Lord.
    1-3 He is my light and salvation amid evildoers.
    4-6 I want to live with him and enjoy his goodness.
7-14 I am also distressed.
    7-10 Hear my prayer; do not forsake me.
    11-12 Lead me through the conflicts I am experiencing.
    13-14 Trusting you while I wait gives me courage.

Notes
- Lament
- "His tent" (v. 6) — David pitched this for the ark on Mount Zion. (See 2 Samuel 6:17.)
- "The house of the Lord" (v. 4). This is not merely the tabernacle; it also suggests that we are God's guests here, who can enjoy his protecting care and goodness in all of life.

For Reflection
- How does God lighten our dark times of danger, trouble, or anxiety?
- "To behold the beauty of the Lord" suggests gazing with wonder and contemplation at the character of God and his redeeming

ways with us. How often should I do this? What will be the effect on me?
- "What worship means is the submission of the whole being to the object of worship. It is the opening of the heart to receive the love of God; it is the subjection of conscience to be directed by Him; it is the declaration of need to be fulfilled by Him; it is the subjection of desire to be controlled by Him; and as the result of all these together, it is the surrender of will to be used by Him. It is the total giving of self."[1]
- "Waiting" — a good word for faith in God. Why?

Prayer
Lord God, what a great light and salvation you were to your beloved Son, even when his adversaries rose up and his followers forsook him. In our time of danger and anxiety, grant us courage to trust and wait, knowing we are guests of a good and gracious Father, Son, and Holy Spirit all the way. Amen.

---

1. William Temple, *Daily Readings from William Temple*, #108 (London: Hodder and Stoughton, 1951).

28
To You, O Lord, I Call

Do not drag me away with the wicked ...
  they do not regard the works of the Lord,
  or the work of his hands ...
O save your people, and bless your heritage;
  be their shepherd, and carry them forever.
— **Psalm 28:3a, 5a, 9**

Theme: A cry for help and a thanksgiving for it

Outline
1-2 Urgent plea for God to hear and speak.
3-5 Do not treat me as you must with the wicked.
6-7 Thanks and praise for answered prayer.
8-9 Concluding intercession for the people.

Notes
- Lament
- Verse 4 is not a plea for revenge but for God to end their evil doing. The revelation of God shows him as one who mercifully breaks down (judges) the evil in order to redeem and rebuild.
- Unbelief (practical atheism) is the root of the evil doings (v. 5).

For Reflection
- Is this simple but great confession of faith (v. 7) also the resolve of my heart?

Prayer
O God, if you were silent to us, we would be on that downward slope. But you speak to us in your Word, our Lord Jesus Christ. Continue to shepherd us and carry us to joy and exultation in you forever. Amen.

29
Ascribe To The Lord, O Heavenly Beings

Ascribe to the Lord glory and strength ...
worship the Lord in holy splendor ...
the God of glory thunders ...
The voice of the Lord shakes the wilderness ...
and in his temple all say "Glory!"
— **Psalm 29:1b, 2b, 3b, 8a, 9b**

Theme: The voice of God in a great storm

Outline

1-2   The heavenly beings are called to praise Yahweh.
3-9   The occasion: the thunder of his voice convulses nature, proclaims his power, and the angels chant, "Glory!"
10-11 But his people need not fear. His strength is shown in blessing his people with peace.

Notes
- Creation
- "The waters ... mighty waters" probably meaning the ocean (vv. 3-4) are a symbol to Israel of great danger, even evil (the flood, Red Sea, and so on).
- Sirion was the old name of majestic Mount Hermon (v. 6).
- "Strip the forests bare" could also mean to cause the deer to go into labor (v. 9).
- Peace (Shalom) includes material and spiritual blessings (v. 10), "every good and perfect gift" (James 1:17) for the well-being of his people.

For Reflection
- This example of theological and poetic interpretation of a storm encourages us to see the Creator's power in all the awesome beauties and wonders of nature. And this gives us occasion to be praising God every day! (For violent storms we could read Psalm 27; 31; or 121.)

Prayer
O God, your heavenly beings sang one night to poor "shepherds abiding in the field," and their song was "Glory to God" and your shalom for the earth and its inhabitants. Through all kinds of storms, may we see you enthroned above them and bringing fullness of life to us in your Son, Jesus Christ our Lord. Amen.

30
I Will Extol You, O Lord

O Lord, my God, I cried to you for help,
*   and you have healed me ...*
As for me, I said in my prosperity,
*   "I shall never be moved" ...*
*   you hid your face; I was dismayed.*
"What profit is there in my death,
*   if I go down to the Pit?*
Will the dust praise you? ...
You have turned my mourning into dancing."
— Psalm 30:2, 6, 7b, 9a, 11a

Theme: Thanksgiving for recovery from critical illness

Outline
1-3   Thanks to the Lord for healing and for deliverance from death.
4-5   Let the faithful praise him, too.
6-7   His experience: his smugness needed correction.
8-10   Death is such a waste!
11-12 His life is prolonged for the praise of God.

Notes
- Thanksgiving
- Death (See note on Psalm 6.) Unlike pagans, the psalmists do not look on death as a release to be welcomed, because they knew life with God is good. He made us and cares for us. Knowing Yahweh, his great redeeming works and steadfast covenant love prompt the hunger for something better than death to be revealed.

For Reflection
- What are we here for? Why should God prolong one's life? What purpose can sickness have? What purpose can healing have?

Prayer
Lord God, for the gift of life in all its goodness we praise you. But even more we praise you for the promise that sorrow and death shall not take from us the glorious opportunity to live for you with joys eternal, through Jesus Christ our Lord. Amen.

31
In You, O LORD, I Seek Refuge

... in your righteousness deliver me ...
take me out of the net that is hidden for me,
for you are my refuge.
Into your hand I commit my spirit;
you have redeemed me, O LORD, faithful God ...
My times are in your hand.
— Psalm 31:1b, 4, 5, 15a

Theme: Protected and preserved by the LORD

Outline
1-8   Beginning with a plea for deliverance, he remembers with joy God's past mercies to him.
9-18 Once again his need is extremely urgent.
19-24 Looking back on his faint-heartedness, he praises God with grateful joy for having preserved him, telling us to take courage!

Notes
- Lament
- "In your righteousness deliver me" (v. 1) — This phrase deeply disturbed Luther as he was preparing a summary of this psalm. He thought of it as punitive and condemning, until he read of it in Romans, where Saint Paul speaks of it as "rather the forgiving righteousness of God by which in his mercy he makes us just" (righteous). Luther discovered the gospel! "As much as I had heretofore hated the words 'righteousness of God,' so much the more dear and sweet it was to me now."[1]

For Reflection
- Verse 5 includes a prayer Jesus learned probably from childhood. He prayed it in his last breath. From his example many famous Christians have prayed it at the approach of death: Saint Basil, Saint Bernard, Huss, Luther, Melancthon, and surely, countless others!

- "My times are in your hand" (vv. 14-15) are great words to remember when confronted with threats, omens, fortune-telling, the occult, and even hypochondria.

Prayer

You are a mighty fortress, O God, for all who take refuge in your forgiving righteousness. In all the troubles of heart and life, we will take courage in knowing our times are in your redeeming hands. We rejoice with anticipation for the abundant goodness you have laid up for us in Jesus Christ, your Son, our Lord. Amen.

---

1. Heinrich Boehmer, *Road to Reformation! Martin Luther to the Year 1521* (Philadelphia: The Muhlenberg Press, 1946), p. 111.

32
Happy Are Those Whose Transgression Is Forgiven

Happy are those whose transgression is forgiven,
  whose sin is covered.
*Happy are those to whom the L*ORD *imputes no iniquity*
  and in whose spirit there is no deceit ...
*I said, "I will confess my transgressions to the L*ORD*,"*
  and you forgave the guilt of my sin.
                                    — **Psalm 32:1, 2, 5b**

Theme: The joy of forgiveness

Outline
David speaks of God's forgiving him.
1-2   What a great blessing it was to have God's forgiveness of my sin.
3-5   How miserable I was until I confessed.
6-7   Pray to God in your distress.
8-10 Then follow the guidance of the LORD.
11   And rejoice in the LORD with me!

Notes
- Penitential
- The Penitential Psalms are 6; 32; 38; 51; 102; 130; 143.
- After being convicted of his sin by the prophet Nathan, David probably expressed his penitence in Psalm 51, and then again, later, in this psalm.
- Proverbs 28:13 and 1 John 1:8-9.
- In verse 11, the forgiven one is called "righteous" because God regards him as holy. (See Romans 4:6 and 8:30.)
- This was one of Saint Augustine's favorite psalms. He had it written on the wall so he could be comforted by it while sick and awaiting death.

For Reflection
Note how David describes
1. the torments of a guilty conscience;
2. the condition of forgiveness;
3. the blessings the forgiven one may enjoy; and
4. two conditions for this joy, in verses 5-11.

Prayer
When we are troubled by our guilt, O Lord, feeling your heavy hand on us, prompt us to confess it all before you. Let that covering or atonement you in mercy provided for us be the ground of our joy and confidence in life and in death. All praise to you for him who was wounded for our transgressions and bruised for our iniquities, our Lord Jesus Christ. Amen.

33
Rejoice In The LORD

Rejoice in the LORD, O you righteous.
Praise befits the upright ...
For the word of the LORD is upright,
and all his work is done in faithfulness ...
let all the inhabitants of the world
stand in awe of him.
For he spoke, and it came to be ...
Our heart is glad in him,
because we trust in his holy name.
— **Psalm 33:1, 4, 8b, 9a, 21**

Theme: How fitting it is to praise Yahweh!

Outline
1-3   Call to praise God.
4-19 Reasons why praise of God is fitting:
    4-5   his character,
    6-9   his creative power,
    10-11 his sovereign rule,
    12-15 his chosen people among the nations, and
    16-19 his protection far better than the might of man.
20-22 We confess our faith and trust in him

Notes
- Praise — Creation/History

For Reflection
- History is full of surprises and mysteries. Among them one can find examples of the truths in verses 10-19, reminding us that our ultimate security rests not with physical might, nor scientific know-how, nor in the wisdom and plans of humankind, but in the Lord and his purpose. Is this widely believed today? How can we be bold proclaimers of it in our day?
- Read Ephesians 1:9-12 (or Colossians 1:15-20) for a good follow-up to this psalm.

Prayer
With awe we praise you, Lord God, for creating the heavens and the earth. But even more we praise you for your continued care and work to accomplish your heart's desire among us all. We wait with trust and gladness for the great fulfillment, which will come through your Word, the Lord Jesus Christ. Amen.

34
I Will Bless The Lord At All Times

... his praise shall continually be in my mouth ...
I sought the Lord, and he answered me,
*   and delivered me from all my fears ...*
O taste and see that the Lord is good;
*   happy are those who take refuge in him ...*
Come, O children ...
I will teach you the fear of the Lord.
Many are the afflictions of the righteous,
*   but the Lord rescues them from them all.*
        — **Psalm 34:1b, 4, 8, 11, 19**

Theme: Praise him who delivers us from evil

Outline
1-10   Let's celebrate the Lord's care for us.
11-22   Let's learn well the "fear" of the Lord.

Notes
- Thanksgiving — Alphabetical
- The suggestion by the ancient title is of an occasion in the life of David told in Samuel 21:11 ff.
- Similarities with the book of Proverbs, which was written after David's time.
- "The fear of the Lord" (v. 11): A better word than fear is awe. The psalmist equates it with faithfulness to the covenant, devotion to God, trust and obedience.
- It has been defined as "a trembling adoration of the transcendent holy Lord," a wholesome reverence, even dread. It appears to be the effect of the experience of God's holy otherness in contrast to our sinfulness, anxiety, uneasy conscience, and divided loyalties.[1]

For Reflection
- Praise is an attitude, inward gratitude, and awe occurring in the midst of a busy life (v. 1). Our words of praise are like the tip of the iceberg compared to the unseen part.

- We are invited to make a personal trial of the way of faith (v. 8). Especially encouraged are the humble(d) (vv. 2, 6, 18).

Prayer
Teach us, Lord God, to fear you in the right way, dreading to offend or grieve you. May we seek your redeeming love to bring us through all trials and afflictions unto yourself with a joy no one can take from us, through Jesus Christ, your Son, our Lord. Amen.

---

1. Alan Richardson, *A Theological Wordbook of the Bible* (New York: Macmillan, 1951), p. 81.

35
Contend, O LORD, With Those Who Contend With Me

Contend, O Lord, with those who contend with me;
   fight against those who fight against me!
Say to my soul,
   "I am your salvation."
Let them be put to shame and dishonor
   who seek after my life ...
Then my soul shall rejoice in the LORD,
   exulting in his deliverance.
   — **Psalm 35:1, 3b-4a, 9**

Theme: Do something about my enemies!

Outline
Three Laments
1-8   Fight those who are fighting me! Let them fall!
9-10   I will rejoice in you.
11-17 See their ingratitude and malicious slander. Rescue me!
18   I will thank and praise you.
19-26 Rescue me from those who hate me without cause.
27-28 I will tell of your greatness all day long.

Notes
- Imprecatory
- See 1 Samuel 19-20; 24; and 26 to read of David's conflict with Saul.
- This is one of six Imprecatory Psalms (35; 59; 60; 109; 137; 140).
- In reading Imprecatory Psalms it is helpful to realize that in many times and places of the world, people experience severe oppression, persecution, slander, malice of all kinds, and do not have the resource of our justice system. "Just to express trust in God in such terrible extremities is in very fact an act of praise."[1]

For Reflection
- For the larger vision of dealing with enemies, read Proverbs 24:17; 25:21, and then Matthew 5:43-48; Luke 6:27 ff; and Romans 12:20.

Prayer
Lord God, your Son was slandered and mocked, and his great love was repaid with evil. You came to his defense and exalted him as Lord. May your church follow his example, seeking for all your reign of justice, forgiveness and new life in Jesus Christ our Lord. Amen.

---

1. George A. F. Knight, *Psalms*, Vol. I and II (Philadelphia: Westminster Press, 1982), p. 171.

36
Transgression Speaks To The Wicked

Transgression speaks to the wicked deep in their hearts;
  there is no fear of God before their eyes ...
How precious is your steadfast love, O God!
  All people may take refuge in the shadow of your wings.
They feast on the abundance of your house,
  and you give them drink from the river of your delights.
For with you is the fountain of life;
  in your light we see light.

— Psalm 36:1, 7-9

Theme: The perversity of the rebel and the great goodness of God

Outline
1-4   Lament over the perverse character of the rebellious.
5-9   Adoration of the character of the righteous God.
10-12 Prayer for blessing and protection.

Notes
- Mixed
- Transgression (*pesha*) means rebellion, suggesting apostasy or willful disregard for the covenant (v. 1). Paul quotes verse 1 in Romans 3, where he says all have sinned, no one is righteous, and his grace in Christ is for everyone.
- A good description of practical atheism, the idea of no accountability for one's life and action (v. 2). This is pathetic especially in the unlikelihood of a conviction of sin and repentance.
- Key words about God: steadfast love (*hesed*) = loyal covenanted love; faithfulness (*emunah*) = his complete reliability, never false; righteousness (*tsedeq*) = doing what is right, fair, and just; and judgment (*mishpat*) = ably administering justice (vv. 5-6). (Note: God's care is for the animals, too!)

For Reflection
- Verses 7-9 are among the most beautiful words in the Psalter. A hymn of adoration of God for "all people" to know and enjoy.
- For God's incomparable bounty, read John 4:13-14 and 7:37-39.

Prayer
We pray that all people may come to know you, Lord God, and, renouncing the ways of sin, may feast on the abundance of your house, drink from the river of your delights, and partake of the fountain of life, Jesus Christ, your Son, our Lord. Amen.

37
Do Not Fret Because Of The Wicked

Do not fret because of the wicked;
do not be envious of wrongdoers,
for they will soon fade like the grass ...
Take delight in the LORD,
and he will give you the desires of your heart.
Commit your way to the LORD;
trust in him, and he will act ...
Be still before the LORD and wait patiently for him ...
though we stumble, we shall not fall headlong,
for the Lord holds us by the hand.
— **Psalm 37:1-2a, 4-5, 7a, 24**

Theme: The righteous are rewarded and the wicked are punished

Outline
1-11   In temptation, trust the Lord and do not complain.
12-20 Triumph of the wicked is short-lived.
21-31 God will care for the righteous.
32-40 Retribution is coming for the wicked and reward for the righteous.

Notes
- Wisdom — Acrostic
- This psalm should be interpreted in the light of Psalm 73 and the book of Job. (See also Mark 10:30 and 1 Timothy 4:8.)

For Reflection
- Introducing his beautiful exposition of this psalm, Luther writes: "To comfort those who are impatient because the wicked do evil and yet remain unpunished and very fortunate for so long."
- "Look, here you have this comforting promise: 'He will give you all that your heart desires.' What more do you want?" (vv. 5-6). "But commit your ways, your work, your word, and your walking to God, and do not be bothered by (the wicked). Committing our way to God does not mean that we do nothing. It means that though the hypocrites may denounce, ridicule, slander, or frustrate what we do, we must not give in to them or quit,

but keep right on with it, letting them have their stubbornness and entrusting the whole cause to God, who will make it come out right on both sides."[1]

Prayer
Lord Jesus, you said, "Blessed are the poor" and you were willing to be one of them, finding life good day by day under the Father's love and will. Even to your last breath on the cross, you trusted him, and he fulfilled his righteous promise, raising you and exalting you as Lord of all. Teach us to so trust him, too. Amen.

---

1. Martin Luther, *Luther's Works* Vol. 14 (St. Louis: Concordia Publishing House, 1973), pp. 211-213.

38
O Lord, Do Not Rebuke Me In Your Anger

O Lord, do not rebuke me in your anger,
*   or discipline me in your wrath ...*
There is no soundness in my flesh ...
*   because of my sin.*
O Lord, all my longing is known to you;
*   my sighing is not hidden from you ...*
But it is for you, O Lord, that I wait;
*   it is you, O Lord, my God, who will answer ...*
I confess my iniquity;
*   I am sorry for my sin ...*
make haste to help me,
*   O Lord, my salvation.*
                          — **Psalm 38:1, 3, 9, 15, 18, 22**

Theme: Pleading for healing, the sinner throws himself on God

Outline

1-8   Help! I'm suffering physically and mentally.
9-14   Help! Deserted by friends, threatened by foes.
15-22 Help! I confess my sin. Make haste to help me.

Notes
- Penitential
- The third of the seven penitential psalms.

For Reflection
- In the three divisions of the psalm, do you discern a progress or development in the prayer?
- For which of the following is the prayer fitting? A devout person who is ill and is assumed by others to have sinned? A devout person who has noticeably fallen? A drug-addict, a drunkard, a sexual profligate, a pederast, or a felon, feeling self-loathing? Someone dying and anxious? A Christian at worship who, identifying with the sufferer, says, "There but for the grace of God go I"?

Prayer

Throw away thy rod,
Throw away thy wrath;
O my God,
Take the gentle path.

For my heart's desire
Unto thine is bent:
I aspire
To a full consent.

Though I fail, I weep:
Though I halt in pace,
Yet I creep
To the throne of grace.

Then let wrath remove;
Love will do the deed;
For with love
Stony hearts will bleed.
— **From "Discipline" by George Herbert, d. 1633**

39
I Said, "I Will Guard My Ways"

I held my peace to no avail;
my distress grew worse ...
"LORD, let me know my end,
   and what is the measure of my days;
   let me know how fleeting my life is ...
And now, O Lord, what do I wait for?
   My hope is in you ...
   do not hold your peace at my tears.
For I am your passing guest,
   an alien, like all my forebears...."
— **Psalm 39:2b, 4, 7, 12b**

Theme: Trusting God without assurance

Outline

1-3   Tempted to complain, I kept silent as long as I could.
4-7   Lord, life is short and treasures are fleeting, but my hope is in you.
8-13 Forgive me and give me relief, so that I, your passing guest, may smile again!

Notes
- Lament
- This is a sequel to the preceding psalm.
- The biblical scholar, Heinrich Ewald, says this psalm is "indisputably the most beautiful of all the elegies in the psalter."
- A good prayer for the depressed or despondent.
- Notice his self-restraint in order to uphold the faith in a world of wickedness (v. 1b).

For Reflection
- A sad psalm by one on the edge of despair. But it is a cry of faith, still calling on God, exhibiting restraint in his words (v. 1), acknowledging his sin (v. 8).
- The psalmist was not given a hope of life beyond death, God did not reveal this part of his plan until Christ came. (See 1 John 5:13; John 17:3; and 2 Timothy 1:9-10.)

- Why does the psalmist still hope? Is faith in the Lord a kind of insurance policy, or is it a means to a living fellowship with him? (See 1 Thessalonians 5:9-11.)

Prayer

O God, when we are depressed or despondent, give us faith to share it with you in prayer, like the psalmist did. When our hopes are dashed, our expectations are still of your grace and power to redeem us for eternal life with you, through Jesus Christ our Lord. Amen.

40
I Waited Patiently For The LORD

I waited patiently for the LORD;
  he inclined to me and heard my cry.
He drew me up from the desolate pit ...
  set my feet upon a rock,
  making my steps secure.
He put a new song in my mouth ...
I have not hidden your saving help within my heart,
I have spoken of your faithfulness and your salvation.
  — **Psalm 40:1-3a, 10a**

Theme: Praise for deliverance and prayer for help

Outline

1-3   I waited patiently, and God bent down to me and lifted me out of the mire. Praise him!

4-5   Happiness comes from trusting God and learning of his incomparable goodness.

6-8   Instead of ritual devotion, Lord, you've enabled me to listen to your Word, and I gladly give myself to obey it.

9-10 I have openly proclaimed the glad news of your salvation.

11-12 Evils are always around and sin is always part of me, so stand by me faithfully with your love.

13-17 Protect us from the wicked, so your people, poor and needy, may rejoice in you.

Notes
- Thanksgiving — Lament
- Verses 13-17 recur with slight variation as Psalm 70.
- Verses 6-8 are quoted in Hebrews 10:5-7, using the psalmist's words as prophetic of Christ's offering himself on the cross (far better than the inefficacious sacrifices of the law).
- Read Ephesians 2:1-10 to see how Christians share David's experience of the love of God.

For Reflection
- A worthy objective for the preacher of the word to keep before him as he prepares to teach and preach (vv. 9-10). Couldn't this

psalm be the life story of a faithful Christian — pastor, Sunday school teacher, parent, and so on?
- "I waited patiently" (v. 1). We want God to hurry up! The whole Bible story reminds us that we live by God's timetable. The waiting is productive in developing patience, the persistence and steadfastness in the face of adverse circumstances, the forbearance and forgiveness of wrongs done to us without seeking vengeance.

Prayer
Lord God, you came down to us in your Son, Jesus Christ, lifting us sinners out of our hopeless condition, enabling us to serve you with self-giving and with praise. May your Spirit give us patience to run the race that is set before us, generously sharing the gospel, so that all may know your redeeming love. We praise you, Father, Son, and Holy Spirit. Amen.

41
Happy Are Those Who Consider The Poor

Happy are those who consider the poor;
the LORD *delivers them in the day of trouble.*
The LORD *protects them and keeps them alive;*
They are called happy in the land ...
As for me, I said, "O LORD, *be gracious to me;*
heal me, for I have sinned against you" ...
Blessed be the LORD, *the God of Israel,*
from everlasting to everlasting. Amen and Amen.
— **Psalm 41:1-2a, 4, 13**

Theme: Blessed are the merciful, for they will receive mercy

Outline
1-3   David takes hope and assurance in God's mercy to the merciful.
4-9   Sick and near death, he knows his enemies hope for the worst for him, and even a friend has turned against him.
10-12 He prays for God to raise him up, and to set him in his presence forever.
13   Doxology ending Book One of the psalter.

Notes
- Thanksgiving — Lament, also Suffering Messiah
- Book One of the psalter began with a beatitude, "Happy (blessed) are those ... " and now ends with this psalm, "Happy are those...."
- David's situation here may be that told in 2 Samuel 15-17. Though not mentioned in 2 Samuel, illness may have prevented David from attending to duties and so occasioned the unrest evidenced by Absalom's rebellion. The false friend was likely Ahithophel, his wise and trusted counselor. (See 2 Samuel 15:30-31; 16:15-19; and 17:21-23.)
- Poor can also mean weak or sick. Note the reasons David in his illness finds assurance and hope (vv. 1-3).
- A vivid description of the visitors to the sick king (v. 6).
- "Repay them" (v. 10) — to take vengeance? Probably not, for David refrained from that as, for example 1 Samuel 25:33 and

2 Samuel 3:37-39. It was probably to punish the traitors who had turned against him, God's appointed king.
- See John 13:1-8 where Christ quotes it as a prophecy of his betrayal.

For Reflection
- This psalm, familiar to our Lord, was one of his prayers. How is each verse or section applicable to him? How does he "fill full" each part of the psalm?

Prayer
Lord Jesus, you promised blessings to those who, with you, love the poor, the broken, and the powerless. When you were hated by enemies, betrayed by a friend, you sought only the Father's will and favor, and he raised you and exalted you forever. Bring us poor and broken ones into his presence with you. Amen.

Book Two
Psalms 42 through 72

42
As A Deer Longs For Flowing Streams

My soul thirsts for God,
for the living God.
When shall I come and behold
the face of God?
My tears have been my food day and night,
while people say to me continually,
"Where is your God?" ...
Why are you cast down, O my soul ...
Hope in God; for I shall again praise him,
my help and my God.
— **Psalm 42:2-3, 5**

Theme: Homesick for the house of God

Outline
A poem in three stanzas:
1-5   Stanza 1
          1-2   Yearning for God.
          3-4   Memories of great worship times.
          5   Refrain: Hope in God; he answers my prayers.
6-11   Stanza 2
          6-8   Past blessings a stark contrast to present trouble.
          9-10   The scoffs of unbelievers hurt!
          11   Refrain (as in v. 5).
Psalm 43 Stanza 3

Notes
- Lament
- This psalm begins Book Two (42-72), a collection using Elohim as the name of God (translated "God"), not the proper name, Yahweh (translated "Lord"). It was written by the Levitical family of the Korahites, who had duties in the tabernacle/temple, among whom were temple musicians. (See 1 Chronicles 6:31-33 ff.)
- Psalm 42-43 are a single poem in three stanzas, each ending with the same refrain.

- The writer living near Mount Hermon (v. 6), among heathens who taunted him for his faith (vv. 9-10), is homesick for Jerusalem and the temple, where he would lead processions in festivals (v. 4).
- "Waves and billows" (v. 7) = one trouble after another!

For Reflection
- Many Christians get discouraged when they encounter unbelief or disdain for their faith. What did the psalmist do to find support and relief from his depression?
- Why is corporate worship such a precious and important experience?

Prayer
Lord Jesus, when people look down on us for our faith in you, when troubles pile up and we feel forgotten, when we cannot snap out of our downcast mood, may your Holy Spirit recall us to joys you have given us in the past, and enable us to continue to gather with others to worship you — Father, Son, and Holy Spirit. Amen.

43
Vindicate Me, O God, And Defend My Cause

O send out your light and your truth;
 let them lead me;
let them bring me to your holy hill
 and to your dwelling.
Then I will go to the altar of God,
 to God my exceeding joy;
and I will praise you with the harp,
 O God, my God.
— **Psalm 43:3-4**

Theme: Lead me to you — my true home!

Outline
1-2 Prayer for God to deliver him from insolent and ungodly enemies.
3-4 Prayer to be restored to public worship at God's dwelling-place (temple).
5 "Hope in God; for I shall again praise him."

Notes
- Lament
- See those of the preceding psalm.

For Reflection
- Light and truth are from God — and for what purpose?
- When "cast down," what is to be our example and action?
- How much do we appreciate and make good use of our privilege of corporate worship? List some of the blessings of the Spirit that come from "going to church."
- The poet, George Herbert, says that when the sermon doesn't strike us, then the Holy Spirit is preaching patience to us!

Prayer
Heavenly Father, let your Spirit shine the light of your word into the hearts and lives of pastors and people, that together we may praise you with a joyful and loving witness to the redemption that is in Jesus Christ our Lord. Amen.

44
We Have Heard With Our Ears, O God

We have heard with our ears, O God,
  our ancestors have told us,
what deeds you performed in their days ...
In God we have boasted continually ...
Yet you have rejected us and abased us ...
Because of you we are being killed all day long,
  and accounted as sheep for the slaughter ...
Rise up, and come to our help.
Redeem us for the sake of your steadfast love.
  — Psalm 44:1, 8a, 9a, 22, 26

Theme: A defeated nation cries out to God

Outline
1-3   We have been told of your mighty acts in days of old.
4-8   It was you who brought us those victories.
9-16 But now you've humiliated us!
17-22 We really don't deserve this.
23-26 Wake up! Do not cast us off forever!

Notes
- National Lament
- Israel has often been a victorious warrior. Now she must serve God in defeat — a suffering servant!

For Reflection
- Passing on the Bible stories is still extremely important (v. 1). Why?
- Are there times when defeat, not victory, is the will of God? (v. 9). Or, is God always "on our side"? If so, in what way?
- "There is a time for every matter under heaven ..." says the preacher (Ecclesiastes 3:1). For defeat and humiliation, too? If so, why?
- When our expectations of God are disappointed, what are we to do? When faith and circumstances are in conflict, and we cannot understand God's dealing, what are we to do? What did the psalmist do?

- What does God ask of us — success or faithfulness?

Prayer
Lord God, your prophets and apostles have told us the wondrous deeds you have performed. Your power and your love are greater than all the forces of the universe. Forgive us for trusting in armaments and war more than we trust you and your mysterious ways. Give us love of truth and the faith and humility to live with it, until you bring us to that glorious day of Christ, our Lord, who lives and reigns with you and the Holy Spirit forever. Amen.

45
My Heart Overflows With A Goodly Theme

I address my verses to the king ...
In your majesty ride on victoriously
    for the cause of truth and to defend the right ...
You love righteousness and hate wickedness.
Therefore God, your God, has anointed you
    with the oil of gladness beyond your companions ...
I will cause your name to be celebrated
    in all generations;
        therefore the peoples will praise you forever and ever.
                  — Psalm 45:1b, 4, 6a, 17

Theme: A royal wedding song

Outline

1-9		Addressing the king.
	2-5	You are handsome, of gracious speech, a great warrior.
	6-7a	Your reign is stable, marked by equity and righteousness.
	7b-9	God has blessed you richly.
10-13a		Addressing the queen: devote yourself wholly to the king.
13b-15		Procession to the palace.
16-17		All future generations will celebrate the king!

Notes
- Royal Messianic
- A poem originally written for the king on the occasion of his marriage to a foreign princess.
- Its Messianic significance has been recognized by Jews and Christians. Jewish interpreters regarded it an allegory of the Messiah and Israel, his bride. Christians interpret the king as a type of Christ and the church as his bride. Bonhoeffer says the psalm is "The song and prayer of the love between Jesus, the king, and his church, which belongs to him."[1]
- Verses 6-7 are cited in Hebrews 1:8-9 as a prophecy of Christ's superiority to angels.

- Luther has 104 pages of exposition on this one psalm! "We want to teach and hear something joyful. Therefore I have taken up Psalm 45 in which we shall see how fluent a speaker the Holy Spirit is, who is able to express and picture one and the selfsame thing in various ways."[2]

Prayer
Lord God, you have given us your Son to be our king and made us a part of the church, his bride. Bless your whole church on earth with the love and faith to show the world the glory of the king who is the Lamb, Jesus Christ our Lord. Amen.

---

1. Dietrich Bonhoeffer, *Psalms: The Prayerbook of the Bible* (Minneapolis: Augsburg, 1970), p. 39.

2. Martin Luther, *Luther's Works*, Vol. 12 (St. Louis: Concordia Publishing House, 1973), p. 197.

46
God Is Our Refuge And Strength

God is our refuge and strength,
  a very present help in trouble.
Therefore we will not fear, though the earth should change ...
The nations are in an uproar,
  the kingdoms totter;
  he utters his voice, the earth melts ...
Be still and know that I am God! ...
The Lord of hosts is with us;
  the God of Jacob is our refuge.
                    — **Psalm 46:1-2a, 6, 10a, 11**

Theme: God's rule is supreme over all the earth

Outline

1-3 Even if the earth is convulsed, God's people need not fear, living under his protection.
4-5 God's presence with us is like a river flowing with joy and new life.
6-7 When nations threaten, God is our refuge.
10-11 Yahweh, God of Jacob, is absolute, supreme, our refuge and hope for the all the earth.

Notes
- Affirmation of Faith
- Psalms 46; 47; and 48 are a trilogy of praise for a great deliverance. (See 2 Kings 18-19 and Isaiah 37.)
- Luther wrote the hymn, "A Mighty Fortress," inspired by this psalm.

For Reflection
- In view of wars, conflagrations, environmental disasters, social breakdown, and nuclear threat, this psalm speaks with fresh relevance. What is the proper response to such assurance of God's sovereign power and love? (vv. 2, 4, 8, 10).
- Can the theme of this psalm be misused? The people of Jeremiah's day apparently thought that the temple (sacramental

presence of God in their midst) was enough to assure their security, without taking seriously the warnings of the prophet. (See Jeremiah 7:1-5. See John 2:19-22 for the meaning and fulfillment of the temple.)
- Does being comforted by the assurance of our security with God encourage quietist indifference to the urgent challenges of political or environmental or international issues?

Prayer
Lord God, our refuge and strength, in this world of natural disasters, social breakdown, and international conflict, let not your people's love grow cold and indifferent. Let your Holy Spirit lead us daily to be workers for peace as we partake of the joyful new life in that river called "grace," flowing to us from the throne of the Lamb, Jesus Christ our Lord. Amen.

47
Clap Your Hands, All You Peoples

Clap your hands, all you peoples;
shout to God with loud songs of joy.
*For the L*ORD*, the Most High, is awesome,*
a great king over all the earth.
God has gone up with a shout,
*the L*ORD *with the sound of a trumpet.*
— **Psalm 47:1-2, 5**

Theme: Yahweh, king of Israel, is king of the world

Outline
1-5   As the king was enthroned with shouts and trumpet sound, so Yahweh, God of Israel, is truly God and king over all the earth.
6-10 Praise God! His sovereignty over the whole world is acknowledged, as peoples of all nations gather before him.

Notes
- Kingship of God/Enthronement
- A Messianic Psalm (see Psalm 2 notes), looking forward to the day when all people acknowledge the Lord as king. From ancient times this psalm has been used on Ascension Day.
- It is the New Year's Day Psalm in the synagogues. It may have been used for an annual festival of recrowning the king (fitting reminder he was not only the Lord's anointed but his rule was subordinate — God is the king). The assembled people would clap, shout, and sing. Verse 5 may have been spoken as the king ascended to the throne.
- Read 2 Samuel 6:14-15 to get a picture of similar festivity, when David brought the ark of the Lord to Jerusalem "with shouting and the sound of the trumpet."

For Reflection
- From ancient times, this psalm has been used on Ascension Day. Use the psalm as a prayer of adoration of the ascended Jesus Christ. (See Ephesians 1:20-23.)

Prayer
Ascended Lord Jesus, we rejoice in your victory and look forward with longing for the great day when the night of sin and judgment is over, and all peoples are gathered to the heavenly Jerusalem, in holiness, to live and serve and praise you, with the Father and the Holy Spirit, one God, life without end. Amen.

48
Great Is The LORD And Greatly To Be Praised

Great is the LORD and greatly to be praised
  in the city of our God.
His holy mountain, beautiful in elevation,
  is the joy of all the earth,
Mount Zion, in the far north,
  the city of the great King ...
We ponder your steadfast love, O God,
  in the midst of your temple.
— Psalm 48:1-2, 9

Theme: Zion — the city of God!

Outline

1-2   The greatness of Yahweh and the glory of Mount Zion.
3-8   God has shown himself to be Zion's protector.
9-14 Lessons to be learned and told to the children (with a city tour).

Notes
- Praise — Zion
- The trilogy of praise:
  Psalm 46 for the presence of Yahweh in the city.
  Psalm 47 for Yahweh, king of all the earth.
  Psalm 48 for Yahweh, protector of the city.
- The significance of "Zion" grew:
  a. Originally it is the hill on which the temple was later built (2 Samuel 5:7), and then it stood for the temple (Isaiah 8:18).
  b. It became a name for the city of Jerusalem (Psalm 48).
  c. Zion also came to stand for the people of Israel (Psalm 126:1).
  d. Among Christians, it is the symbol of the church, all God's people.
  e. It came to refer to the heavenly city (Hebrews 12:22; Revelation 14:1).
- "Mount Zion in the far north" is a way of saying "Mount Zion is everything and more than the Assyrians claim for their fabled gods" (v. 2).

- Sennacherib's vassal kings entered Judah, then mysteriously withdrew (vv. 4-6). (See Isaiah 18-19.)

For Reflection And Prayer
Glories of your name are spoken,
Zion, city of our God;
He whose word cannot be broken
Formed you for his own abode.
On the Rock of Ages founded,
What can shake your sure repose?
With salvation's walls surrounded,
You may smile at all your foes.

Savior, since of Zion's city
I through grace a member am,
Let the world deride or pity,
I will glory in your name.
Fading are the worldlings' pleasures
All their boasted pomp and show;
Solid joys and lasting treasures
None but Zion's children know.
— **John Newton (1725-1807)**

49
Hear This, All You Peoples

Hear this, all you peoples;
give ear, all inhabitants of the world,
both low and high,
rich and poor together ...
Truly no ransom avails for one's life,
there is no price one can give to God for it ...
that one should live on forever
and never see the grave ...
But God will ransom my soul from the power of Sheol,
for he will receive me.
— **Psalm 49:1-2, 7, 9, 15**

Theme: Death is a mystery, and wealth is futile

Outline
1-4   Listen! This is for all humankind of every rank and class.
5-12 Wealth is idolized, but it cannot save from death, when it must all be given up.
13-14 Sheol will be the home of the rich.
15-20 God will ransom the godly from Sheol's power. Therefore be not in awe of the pomp of wealth.

Notes
- Wisdom Poetry
- This psalm's theme is similar to that of Psalms 37 and 73.
- The mystery of death and beyond (v. 15). See notes in Introduction and for Psalms 16; 17; and 73.

For Reflection
- See verses 6, 13, and 18 for how wealth was generally regarded then. Is it the same today, too?
- What perspective must we keep before us as we see ourselves or others getting richer? (vv. 7-9, 10-14, 17-20).
- Where is the true wealth, riches, or real estate that can never lose is value? (v. 16; Matthew 19; 21; Hebrews 13:5). What will keep our material possessions from possessing us?

Prayer
Lord God, may we be taught and prompted by your word and your Spirit to seek our fulfillment not in worldly wealth or power, nor in pomp or status, but to seek and find it in you, and in loving service to one another. Grant this in the name of him who became poor that we might be ransomed from death to live with you forever, Jesus Christ our Lord. Amen.

50
The Mighty One, God The Lord, Speaks

The mighty one, God the Lord,
  speaks and summons the earth ...
  for God himself is judge ...
  for the world and all that is in it is mine ...
Offer to God a sacrifice of thanksgiving,
  and pay your vows to the Most High.
Call on me in the day of trouble;
  I will deliver you, and you shall glorify me ...
  to those who go the right way
  I will show the salvation of God.
  — **Psalm 50:1a, 6b, 12b, 14-15, 23b**

Theme: Acceptable worship is in spirit and in truth

Outline
1-6   God is the judge, Israel is being tried, and the witnesses are the heavens.
7-15 God condemns mere material or formal worship, and wants the offering of the heart.
16-21 Those offering form without inward spirit are rebuked.
22-23 All are being warned and called to worship the right way.

Notes
- Liturgy — Prophetic
- Compare with Isaiah 1:11-20; John 4:24; Micah 6:6-8; and Psalm 51:1 ff.

For Reflection
- A thankful heart is the prerequisite for real worship. This comes to one as a realization of God's grace to us in our need of a Savior. This enables us to repent of sin, to begin a new life, and to come to know true joy. A thankful heart and a concern to obey — what Matthew Henry called "Thanks-living."
- Notice the drama of grace in verse 15:
  Act I: Call on me in the day of trouble (any kind of trouble will qualify).

Act II: I will deliver you (in God's way, in God's time; but it will come).

Act III: You will glorify me (a grateful heart bearing witness).

Prayer

O God, Father, Son, and Holy Spirit, your love and grace came first and called us in our baptism and your word to belong to you. We have been forgiven our sins and find new power to reject evil and to seek your good and blessed will for our lives. Continue that good work in us and bring it to completion at the day of Christ our Savior. Amen.

51
Have Mercy On Me, O God

Have mercy on me, O God,
 according to your steadfast love;
according to your abundant mercy
 blot out my transgressions ...
You desire truth in the inward being ...
Create in me a clean heart, O God,
 and put a new and right spirit within me.
Do not cast me away from your presence,
 and do not take your holy spirit from me.
Restore to me the joy of your salvation,
 and sustain in me a willing spirit.
— **Psalm 51:1, 6a, 10-12**

Theme: The greatest of all penitential prayers

Outline
1-2   I am guilty and need mercy.
3-5   I confess my sinfulness.
6   I need inward integrity.
7-12 I need and seek from you:
    7   purging, cleansing,
    8   relief from agony,
    9   the record against me blotted out,
    10   a new creation within me,
    11   your Spirit's presence and ministry, and
    12   a grateful, obedient spirit.
13-15 I commit myself to tell others of your grace.
16-17 All I can offer is a broken spirit.
18-19 Later addition — when the psalm was used by exiles who had returned home. (See Ezra 6:16.)

Notes
- Penitential
- David's sin with Bathsheba (and Uriah) is told in 2 Samuel 11, and the prophet Nathan's rebuke in 2 Samuel 12. Luther writes: "Here the doctrine of true repentance is set forth before us. There

are two elements in true repentance: recognition of sin and recognition of grace ... the fear of God and trust in mercy ... David is an outstanding example. One by one he broke almost the whole Decalogue. Yet, he would not have acknowledged these sins if Nathan had not come, but would still have wanted to be known as a righteous and holy king ... if Nathan had not come, David might have sinned against the Holy Spirit."[1]

For Reflection
- On what ground does David ask for forgiveness? And what is the condition for receiving it?
- List the things (or verbs of God's work) which, when penitent, we ask God to do with us.
- The words used here for sin are transgression (*pesha*) = rebellion or defection against God, iniquity (*aven*) = depravity of conduct, perverting of right, and error (*chata*) = to miss the mark in life.
- "Create" means not restoring what was before, but to bring into being what was not there and is needed — new heart and spirit from the creative, life-giving power of God. (See Ezekiel 36:25-27.)
- Luther: "Now with us the situation is that Adam must get out and Christ come in, Adam become as nothing, and Christ alone remain and rule. For this reason there is no end of washing and cleansing in this life. For the old Adam, with which we are born, makes sinful and nullifies also the good works, in which we make a start and some progress, if God did not look upon the grace and cleansing which has begun."[2]
- Note how this psalm prefigures (vv. 10-13) the Christian teaching of regeneration (John 3:1-16; 2 Corinthians 5:16-21), sanctification (Romans 6:19; 12:1-2), and mission or witness (Matthew 28:19-20).

Prayer
Almighty God, our heavenly Father, you have made your son's death on the cross the covering for the sins of the whole world and have promised to forgive all who confess their sin and seek your mercy. Give us your Holy Spirit, so that, like David of old, we may seek to

be made new and right inwardly and outwardly, and that we may encourage others to seek your grace and your love in Jesus Christ, your Son, our Lord. Amen.

---

1. Martin Luther, *Luther's Works*, Vol. 12 (St. Louis: Concordia Publishing House, 1973), pp. 305-306.

2. *Ibid*, Vol. 14, p. 167.

52
Why Do You Boast, O Mighty One?

Why do you boast, O mighty one,
  of mischief done against the godly? ...
You love evil more than good ...
But God will break you down forever ...
But I am like a green olive tree
  in the house of God,
I trust in the steadfast love of God
  forever and ever.
— Psalm 52:1a, 3a, 5a, 8

Theme: The fate of the cynic

Outline
1-4   You wicked man, strutting in pride, working treachery and slander!
5-7   God will bring you down, and we gloat in anticipation!
8-9   But I will continue to trust God and thank him for his covenant love and blessings.

Notes
- Lament
- The title suggests the background of the psalm to be the gripping story of when Doeg informed against David to Saul. (See 1 Samuel 21-22.)

For Reflection
- Note the characteristics of the godless bully (vv. 1-4, 7). In contrast, what is David's boast? What is the Christian's boast? (See Galatians 6:14.)

Prayer
Lord God, you will bring down the ungodly pride that boasts in riches. Far be it from us to boast, O God, except in your covenant love, sealed with the blood of Christ. Make us to be like olive trees, rooted and nourished in the love and power of Jesus Christ, your Son, bearing fruit to your glory. Amen.

53
Fools Say In Their Hearts
(This is a slight revision of **Psalm 14**)

Fools say in their hearts, "There is no God." ...
Have they no knowledge, those evildoers ...
There they shall be in great terror ...
When God restores the fortunes of his people,
Jacob will rejoice....

— **Psalm 53:1a, 4a, 5a, 6b**

Theme: Denunciation of godlessness

Outline

1-3   Corruption of humankind comes from failure to seek God.
4   Illustrates their oppression of God's people.
5-6   Terror awaits them, but God brings deliverance for Israel.

Notes
- Liturgy — Prophetic
- This psalm, a slight revision of Psalm 14, is one of a number of indications that the book of Psalms as we have it is a gathering of several shorter collections, created somewhat like our modern hymnals are formed. (See introductory article on p. 13.)

For Reflection
- Some atheism today is dogmatic and militant. Atheists are not the problem as much as the practical atheism of our culture: indifference. Plato said of the "secularism" of his time that it reflected belief that the gods don't exist; or, if they do, they don't care about human affairs; or, if they care, they can be easily appeased with a little sacrifice. Today, that indifference is often expressed by the sentiment that "it doesn't matter what you believe, as along as you're sincere" (or feel good). That nullifies the entire revelation of God to us in the record of Israel and the coming of Christ — a popular form of atheism.

Prayer
Eternal God, you do love me and ask that with all my heart I rely on you in all things. It is your earnest desire to be my God, and I must regard you as God or suffer the loss of eternal salvation. My heart shall neither build on nor rely on anything else, whether it be property, honor, wisdom, power, purity, or any other creation. Amen.
— Herbert Brokering, editor, *Luther's Prayers*, #83
(Minneapolis: Augsburg Publishing House, 1967)

54
Save Me, O God, By Your Name

Save me, O God, by your name,
 and vindicate me by your might ...
For the insolent have risen against me,
 the ruthless seek my life;
 they do not set God before them.
But surely, God is my helper;
 the Lord is the upholder of my life.
— **Psalm 54:1, 3-4**

Theme: Appeal to God, who is just and faithful

Outline
1-3 Appeal to God: "The ruthless seek my life."
4-7 He thanks God, trusting God will defend and avenge him as in the past.

Notes
- Lament
- See 1 Samuel 23:19 and 26:1 ff. Saul was told of David's hiding in his territory.

For Reflection
- "By your name" = your reputation revealed to us through your saving all who trust in you. David relies on the character of God — his goodness and saving grace — for facing daily life and its troubles. Should not this be our confidence and joy at all times?
- How does God's character get slandered in our lives today?

Prayer
As we face each new day, O God, we shall rely on your powerful goodness and grace to uphold us in all our troubles. Let not those who neither know you nor fear your judgment cause our love to grow cold. May your Holy Spirit prompt us to give thanks and praise to you through him who died for the ungodly, Jesus Christ, our risen Lord. Amen.

55
Give Ear To My Prayer, O God

I am troubled in my complaint.
I am distraught by the noise of the enemy ...
My heart is in anguish within me ...
And I say, "O that I had wings like a dove!
I would fly away and be at rest ..."
But I call upon God,
*and the L*ORD *will save me ...*
*Cast your burden on the L*ORD,
and he will sustain you.
— **Psalm 55:2b, 4a, 6, 16, 22a**

Theme: Complaint about a friend's treachery

Outline
1-3a   Urgent prayer in great distress.
3b-5   Its effect on him.
6-8   He longs to escape it all.
9-11   Anger toward the violence and strife in the city.
12-15   Anger toward the faithless friend.
16-22   God will hear and act, sustaining the righteous and casting down the wicked.

Notes
- Lament
- A Messianic Suffering Psalm reminding us of the sufferings of Christ, helping us to feel what he must have felt.
- Some believe the psalm refers to the rebellion of Absalom and the treachery of Ahithophel (2 Samuel 15-16). Some think it could have been Jeremiah's experience and prayer (Jeremiah 5-6). Jerome considered it a foreshadowing of Christ's experience. In his translation of the Bible into Latin (Vulgate), the title says, "The voice of Christ against the chiefs of the Jews and the traitor Judas."
- "Moved" = final, fatal disaster, or permanently distressed, or driven to despair. God will never permit this to happen to the righteous (v. 22).

For Reflection
- Note the vivid description of social and moral breakdown in the city (vv. 9-11), and the deceitful betrayal by an individual (vv. 20-21), and then the effect of it on the psalmist (vv. 2, 3, 4, 17). Of the two ways of meeting trouble (vv. 6-7, 22) which is the better and why?

Prayer
Lord Jesus, you know what it's like to be hemmed in by troubles: rejected by your people and your church, deserted by your disciples, betrayed by a friend, scourged and mocked by soldiers. You never moved from trusting the Father. In our troubles, share your faith with us, and may your Spirit assure us of our salvation now and forever. Amen.

56
Be Gracious To Me, O God

O Most High, when I am afraid,
  I put my trust in you ...
I am not afraid: what can flesh do to me? ...
This I know, that God is for me.
For you have delivered my soul from death,
  and my feet from falling,
so that I may walk before God in the light of life.
— **Psalm 56:2b-3, 9b, 13**

Theme: When in danger, trust in God

Outline
1-2 Foes are trying to crush me.
3-4 But I will trust God whose word I praise.
5-9a They plot evil against me. Cast them down!
9b-13 I will trust and thank God, who saves me.

Notes
- Lament — Messianic Suffering
- From the title, "A Miktam" = probably a musical term with the suggestion it be sung to the tune, "The Dove On Far-Off Terebinth."
- Read 2 Samuel 21:10 ff to learn the suggested background for the psalm. David credits the Lord for saving him (including the effective clever tactics he used to throw off the enemy!).

For Reflection
- In verses 3-4 and 10-11 see the linkage of God's word, faith, and prayer. What is the relation?
- "Walk" = go about one's daily life (v. 13).
- What is the purpose of one's life being spared? (v. 13). (See 1 Thessalonians 5:9-10.)
- "This I know, that God is for me." (See 1 John 4:13-16.) This is better than "God is on our side ... We are Christians, not because we are always right, but because our sins have been forgiven for Christ's sake."[1]

Prayer
Lord God, we are in danger from many foes, physical, moral, and spiritual. In the midst of conflict and trial, enable us to trust in you. Your word assures us you are truly for us, having destined us to live with you now and forever, forgiven and redeemed, through our Lord Jesus Christ. Amen.

---

1. From a lecture by George Forell, Carver Distinguished Professor of Religion, University of Iowa.

57
Be Merciful To Me, O God

Be merciful to me,
  for in you my soul takes refuge;
in the shadow of your wings
  I will take refuge,
  until the destroying storms pass by.
I cry to God Most High,
  to God who fulfills his purpose for me.
He will send from heaven and save me.
— Psalm 57:1-3a

Theme: Amid dangers — praise the Lord!

Outline

1-4   Prayer and confidence in God's protection in the midst of danger.
5   "Glory to God" refrain.
6-10   The malicious tactics of his enemies turn to their own defeat, and with steadfastness he exults in thanks to God, praying for all the earth to behold his glory.
11   "Glory to God" refrain.

Notes
- Lament
- Note poetic repetition for emphasis in verses 1, 3, 7, 8, and the refrain in verses 5 and 11.
- The title refers us to David's experience and courage as told in 1 Samuel 22 or 24.
- The church has used it as a proper psalm for Easter Day, in celebration of Christ's triumph over death and hell, and the Messianic hope expressed in verses 5 and 11.

For Reflection
- What is God's purpose for me? Based on verse 3, his covenant love that he will "send forth." "There is no such thing as love and no such thing as faithfulness; these are merely abstract ideas. Only a living person 'sends forth love.' In other words, God sends

himself, full of steadfast love and loyalty to his faithfulness, that is to his unchangeableness within the covenant."[1]

Prayer
When destroying storms in nature and in the human family threaten us, give to us courage from your promise that you will fulfill your purpose for us: your name hallowed, your kingdom come, and your will for us in Christ fully carried out. May all share in such a fulfillment with us through Christ our Lord. Amen.

---

1. George A. F. Knight, *The Daily Study Bible Series — Psalms*, Vol. 1 (Philadelphia: Westminster Press, 1982), p. 267.

58
Do You Indeed Decree What Is Right, You Gods?

Do you judge people fairly?
No, in your hearts you devise wrongs;
  your hands deal out violence on earth ...
The righteous will rejoice when they see vengeance done; ...
People will say, "Surely there is a reward
  for the righteous;
  surely there is a God who judges on earth."
— Psalm 58:1b-2, 10a, 11

Theme: Prayer for the downfall of evil powers

Outline
1-2 Even those in authority do unjustly!
3-5 They are like the incurably wicked.
6-9 This being the case, render them powerless; may they vanish away!
10-11 The righteous, freed from oppression, will recognize the reality of God's moral government of the world.

Notes
- Lament — Imprecatory

For Reflection
- Dietrich Bonhoeffer said, "What right then have we, we who are ourselves guilty and deserving God's wrath, to call for his vengeance against our enemies, without expecting this same wrath to be called down on us? No, we cannot pray this psalm ... Not because we are much too good to do that ... but because we are too sinful, too bad to do that ... But God has chosen to prepare in David one who will be called the Son of David, Jesus Christ ... Only he who bore the anger of God, only he may ask forgiveness for the godless. Thus he alone has made us free from God's anger and vengeance ... When we behold him, the crucified, we understand God's just and living anger against us godless, and at the same time, the liberation from his anger."[1]

Prayer
Lord Jesus, you have delivered us from the righteous anger and justice of God upon sin. You sought the Father's justice and his purpose to bring his forgiving, restoring love to us through your cross. Enable us to seek your justice to overcome evil by your way of self-giving love, and in your strength. Amen.

---

1. Dietrich Bonhoeffer, *Meditations On Psalms*, ed. Edwin Robertson (Grand Rapids, Michigan: Zondervan, 2002), p. 57 ff.

59
Deliver Me From My Enemies, O God

Deliver me from those who work evil ...
Each evening they come back,
*   howling like dogs,*
*   and prowling about the city ...*
But I will sing of your might ...
*   for you, O God, are my fortress,*
*   the God who shows me steadfast love.*
— **Psalm 59:2a, 14, 16a, 17b**

Theme: Enemies lie in wait, but God is my fortress

Outline

1-5	Protect me from my enemies.
6-9	They threaten insolently, but you will laugh at them!
10-13	Don't punish them right away — let them perish through their pride!
14-17	Though they rage like howling dogs, I will calmly trust in you.

Notes
- Lament
- The title refers us to David's conflict with Saul as told in 1 Samuel 19:8-18. References in the psalm to the nations may be a stanza added to David's prayer when the psalm was adapted for the use of the nation in the temple.

For Reflection
- "The Psalter has much more to say to the world of suffering humanity than you and I can ever grasp in our own small corner in the history of mankind. Narrow-mindedness, ignorance, and self-centeredness are emotions that a study of the psalms themselves can help us to overcome, and in their place give us a concerned, thoughtful, and prayerful view of the kind of life that many of our fellow human beings are condemned to face ... We should remember that the characteristic state of the ordinary man

in any European country in the Middle Ages was one of fear — of (a) the plague, (b) disease, (c) invasion, (d) the tax collector, (e) witchcraft and magic, (f) the unknown, (g) an early death."[1]

Prayer
Lord God, you have shown your power over death and all evil in the cross and resurrection of your Son. Deliver us from evil that we may live to your praise and share with joy your redeeming love, through Jesus Christ our Lord. Amen.

---

1. George A. F. Knight, *The Daily Study Bible Series — Psalms* (Philadelphia: Westminster Press, 1982), pp. 275-276.

60
O God, You Have Rejected Us

O God ... you have made your people
  suffer hard things;
You have given us wine to drink
  that made us reel ...
O grant us help against the foe,
  for human help is worthless.
With God we shall do valiantly;
  it is he who will tread down our foes.
— **Psalm 60:3, 11-12**

Theme: Prayer of a nation in defeat

Outline

1-4   You have let us suffer defeat!
5-8   You promised us dominion over the neighboring nations.
9-12 With you we shall do valiantly.

Notes
- Lament
- The title refers to one of the wars of David that came to disaster (not recorded in 2 Samuel), putting in peril the safety of the kingdom. If so, it was a fitting cry of Israel in later times as well.
- An earlier prophecy had promised a united kingdom and neighbor nations in subjection (vv. 6-8). Proud neighbor, Moab, is compared to the victor's washbasin, defiant Edom to the lowest slave (carrying or cleaning his sandals). Shechem (west of the Jordan) and Succoth (east of the Jordan) were two places associated with Jacob's journeys.
- The compiler of Psalm 108 includes verses 6-12 of this psalm into Psalm 108:7-13.

For Reflection
- To pray to God when we are defeated shows faith in him. Setbacks or defeats can be useful to God for our growing in grace. There are times when we can win by losing, though we may not understand how. Faith waits and continues to place us in the Lord's good hands.

Prayer

Lord Jesus, all authority in heaven and earth has been given to you. When we are defeated and helpless in the face of triumphant evils, give us the faith to remember it is not human help but you who will tread down our foes. Then give us also the courage to stand fast, knowing that nothing shall separate us from your love. Amen.

61
Hear My Cry, O God

From the end of the earth I call to you,
when my heart is faint.
Lead me to the rock
that is higher than I;
for you are my refuge ...
Prolong the life of the king ...
May he be enthroned forever before God;
appoint steadfast love and faithfulness
to watch over him!
— Psalm 61:2, 3a, 6a, 7

Theme: Prayer of an exile

Outline
1-4 Fainthearted, he prays for God to be his security and to return him to God's dwelling-place.
5-8 Grateful for God's hearing his prayer, for his spiritual heritage, and for God's promises to the king, he takes cheer and pledges a life of thanksgiving to God.

Notes
- Royal Messianic — Lament
- This is David's reference to God's anointed (himself), in the third person (vv. 6-7). Probably prayed when leaving Jerusalem during Absalom's rebellion.
- "The rock that is higher than I" = God, and the asylum from enemies he provides (vv. 2, 4). The "tent" = the tabernacle (later temple). God's constancy, changelessness, and protection is what is emphasized by the "rock" metaphor.
- This psalm was later used as a prayer of the nation in its dispersion, and the king was interpreted to be the Messiah.

For Reflection
- This psalm was prayed when David was a fugitive, his throne temporarily occupied by another, and his life was in grave danger. He expresses his heart's desire in those circumstances. What was it?

Prayer

Lord God, when our hearts are faint with fear or doubt, may your Holy Spirit give us good cheer and courage, remind us of your unchanging grace and of the love our king Jesus has for us. May we live in grateful, hope-filled praise to you, Father, Son, and Holy Spirit. Amen.

62
For God Alone My Soul Waits In Silence

For God alone my soul waits in silence;
from him comes my salvation ...
On God rests my deliverance and my honor ...
Trust in him at all times, O people;
pour out your heart before him;
God is a refuge for us.
— **Psalm 62:1, 7a, 8**

Theme: In God alone is our hope and confidence

Outline
1-2   David's faith: God alone is my salvation.
3-4   David's enemies: My enemies, seeing weakness, plot my downfall.
5-7   David's testimony: But I trust God for my deliverance and honor.
8-12 David's counsel to us: So trust him, O people. Not humans high or low, nor wealth, but he alone has the power and the love needed to deliver you.

Notes
- Affirmation of Faith
- The psalm is applicable to many of David's experiences, especially of the time of Absalom's rebellion (2 Samuel 15). (See also 1 Samuel 30:6b.)

For Reflection
- David's counsel is timely for every generation. What in it is especially relevant today?

Prayer
Lord God, everything is changing here, and we feel threatened, longing for peace. We are grateful that you listen to us as we pour out our hearts to you. Trusting you alone, let us not become distracted by wealth or by danger from others. Protect and keep us in your steadfast love through Jesus Christ your Son, our Lord. Amen.

63
O God, You Are My God, I Seek You

O God, you are my God, I seek you,
  my soul thirsts for you;
my flesh faints for you,
  as in a dry and weary land
  where there is no water ...
My soul is satisfied as with a rich feast ...
  when I think of you on my bed,
  and meditate on you in the watches of the night.
                                   — Psalm 63:1, 5a, 6

Theme: Thirsting for God

Outline
1-2   The king's thirst for God.
3   The king's most precious treasure: God's steadfast love.
4-8   The king's grateful joy recalling God's mercy.
9-11 The king's confidence in God for victory.

Notes
- Lament
- The two preceding psalms come to a climax here. Flight from Absalom was probably the occasion. (See 2 Samuel 15.)
- "The king" = David, the psalmist (v. 11).

For Reflection
- David fled Jerusalem and, to all appearances, had lost his kingdom, his throne, and the capital. Yet, he considered God's steadfast love better than all life could offer (v. 3). What did the vision of God in his heart do for him? (vv. 3-11).
- "When will the world of our psalmist break into at least the Christian community, so that we, whether in joy or in sorrow, in hunger, in sickness, in fear and trouble, in sadness and deepest guilt, in good and bad harvests, can say with triumph: 'And though they take our life, goods, honor, children, wife, yet is their profit small; these things shall vanish all, the city of God remains' ... God, your love is better than life."[1]

Prayer
Heavenly Father, teach us by your Spirit and your Word to comprehend with all the saints what is the breadth and length and height and depth, to know the love of Christ that surpasses knowledge, filled with all the fullness of God. Your power is at work within us to accomplish far more than we can ask or imagine, and to you be all the glory forever. Amen.

---

1. Dietrich Bonhoeffer, *Meditations On Psalms*, ed. Edwin Robertson (Grand Rapids, Michigan: Zondervan, 2002), p. 41.

64
Hear My Voice, O God, In My Complaint

Hide me from the secret plots of the wicked,
*   from the scheming of evildoers ...*
But God will shoot his arrow at them ...
*   ... he will bring them to ruin ...*
Then everyone will fear ...
Let the righteous rejoice in the LORD
*   and take refuge in him.*
Let all the upright in heart glory.
                    — Psalm 64:2, 7a, 8a, 9a, 10

Theme: The certainty of God's judgment on the wicked

Outline
1   Protect me, God, from the enemy.
2-6   Hide me from their wicked scheming and slander.
7-11   God will bring them down, and we all will rejoice in him.

Notes
- Lament
- Translations of this psalm differ, due to the corruption of the Hebrew text, but the message is the same.

For Reflection
- Think of all the people through the centuries who have had to live in terror because of conditions of anarchy or a police state. They are powerless against the scheming and slander of the sociopath next door or in powerful office.
- When God does something about wickedness, what are the results one can expect? (Which results show one of God's methods, and which his purpose in judging evil?)
    a. God will act sooner or later, but suddenly (v. 7).
    b. God lets them get caught in their own arrogance and wrong (v. 8).
    c. This leads to a new grasp of faith (v. 9).
    d. Fearing God, people lose their fear of man (v. 9).
    e. They ponder the acts of God — (theology!).

Prayer
Lord God, your judgment upon sin is a fearful thing to consider. You have provided us refuge from it by our union with Christ. We will rejoice in your redeeming love for us, and pray and witness the good news for others, the Spirit directing us in our praise of you, through Jesus Christ our Lord. Amen.

65
Praise Is Due To You, O God, In Zion

Praise is due to you, O God, in Zion ...
　　O you who answer prayer!
To you all flesh shall come ...
You visit the earth and water it,
　　you greatly enrich it ...
　　you provide the people with grain ...
You crown the year with your bounty.
The pastures of the wilderness overflow,
　　the hills gird themselves with joy

— Psalm 65:1a, 2, 9, 11

Theme: Thanksgiving for a great harvest

Outline
1-2　God be praised in Zion and by all humankind.
3-4　For forgiving our sins and welcoming us in your temple,
5　　for your goodness and past deliverances,
6-8　for sustaining and controlling the forces of nature, and
9-13　for the gift of a bountiful harvest. Even the meadows, hills, and valleys sing for joy!

Notes
- Praise — Creation/History
- Picture the worshiping congregation gathered in the temple at the presentation of the firstfruits at the Passover (vv. 9-13). (See Leviticus 23:10-14.)

For Reflection
- This is a beautiful, exuberant poem of praise for a great harvest. Even the earth rejoices! Thus, the faithful had a reverence for the earth, sensing a good relationship, something many of the modern generation do not share. There has been a ruthless exploiting of its value with little thought for its renewal. Worse yet, there is an easy-going acceptance of poverty and hunger in our midst and in many places of the earth.

- Can we work and give and pray for a change of attitude? Whatever our political loyalties, should we not all be environmentalists like the psalmists and the apostles were? (See Romans 8:19-23.)

Prayer

Dear God, you have created a marvelous earth on which we dwell. Your lavish generosity is seen in its beauty and its rich provision sufficient for everyone. Forgive us for indifference toward the poor and hungry of the world. Make us generous toward them with gifts and prayers that those who live at earth's farthest bounds may be fed, cheered by your love, and rejoice in you with us, through your Son, Jesus Christ our Lord. Amen.

66
Make A Joyful Noise To God, All The Earth

Come and see what God has done;
   he is awesome in his deeds among mortals ...
For you, O God, have tested us;
   you have tried us as silver is tried ...
yet you have brought us out to a spacious place ...
Come and hear, all you who fear God,
   and I will tell what he has done for me ...
If I had cherished iniquity in my heart,
   the Lord would not have listened.
But truly God has listened ...
   — **Psalm 66:5, 10, 12b, 16, 18, 19a**

Theme: Israel calls the world to praise God

Outline
1-4   All people! Praise God!
5-7   Come and see his works and his sovereignty.
8-12   He brought us through fire and water to a spacious place.
13-15 I will gratefully pay vows I made in distress.
16-20 Come and hear what God has done for me. Blessed be God!

Notes
- Thanksgiving
- This is a good missions psalm. Note the evangelical appeal to all people.
- Isaiah 36-38 tells a great story that could well be the background of this psalm, and the psalmist could be devout King Hezekiah.

For Reflection
- This is a good prayer for one who has been through a lot of suffering and lives to tell of it. Looking back, the psalmist sees God's care through it all. Pray for God to bring you to this point. It reminds us of Revelation 7:13-17.

- Verses 17-20 provide an insight into one's prayer-life. While this is not the whole explanation of answered prayer, it is a part (v. 20). Grace and forgiveness were the bottom-line experience of the psalmist.

Prayer
Lord God, through all trials and testing, like silver tried in the fire, bring us forth refined in our faith and our loyal commitment to you and to your Son, Jesus Christ our Lord. Lead us to say with the love no experience can destroy, "Blessed be God forever! Blessed be Father, Son, and Holy Spirit." Amen.

67
May God Be Gracious To Us

May God be gracious to us and bless us
and make his face to shine upon us,
that your way may be known upon earth,
your saving power among all nations.
Let the peoples praise you, O God;
let all the peoples praise you.

— Psalm 67:1-3

Theme: A great prayer for missions

Outline
1-2   God bless us so that all the world may come to know the Savior God.
3-4   May all nations come to praise the God of Israel.
5-7   Let all peoples praise God and revere him for the gift of the harvest.

Notes
- Thanksgiving
- A joyful psalm, evangelical in spirit, wanting all people to know the saving power of God.
- Verse echoes the Aaronic benediction (Numbers 6:24 ff).

For Reflection
- This is Israel at its best. Think of how joy and concern for the world's redemption seem to go hand-in-hand. Do we seek God's blessing for this purpose? Or just for ourselves? If Christians have a defeated attitude, could this be part of the problem? The church and the individual Christian need to pray this psalm.
- It would be a good alternative to the Nunc Dimittis to use often!

Prayer
O God, you shine your holiness, love, and glory upon us in Jesus, your Son, in his life, his death, and his resurrection. May this revelation of you bless and make us more effective in our calling to make known your redeeming way to all peoples everywhere. Amen.

68
Let God Rise Up, Let His Enemies Be Scattered

But let the righteous be joyful;
  let them exult before God;
  let them be jubilant with joy ...
Our God is a God of salvation,
  and to God, the Lord, belongs escape from death ...
Sing to God, O kingdoms of the earth ...
  the God of Israel ... gives strength
  to his people.
  — **Psalm 68:3, 20, 32a, 35b**

Theme: The triumphant onward march of God

Outline

1-3	Invocation — The procession begins with a prayer for God to lead on, overcoming his foes and bringing joy to his people.
4-6	Welcome to the Lord! Remember who he is — helper of the helpless and liberator of captives.
7-18	He has shown his power and love in Israel's history:
	7-10 the exodus and entry to promised land,
	11-14 the conquest of Canaan, and
	15-18 the choice of Zion for his earthly dwelling-place.
19-23	God, our redeemer, leads us on and brings enemies to judgment.
24-27	A united Israel will celebrate him.
28-31	Prayer for the day when opposition is subdued and nations turn to God.
32-35	All nations are called to praise Israel's God.

Notes
- Praise — Salvation
- These are words Moses used leading Israel in its journey (v. 1). (See Numbers 10:35.)
- Saint Paul quotes this triumph over Israel's enemies as prefiguring the triumph of Christ over spiritual enemies (v. 18). (See Colossians 2:15.)

- This psalm has been a favorite of the Crusaders; of Italian reformer, Girolamo Savonarola; of the Huguenots; and of Oliver Cromwell.
- This psalm celebrates the history of God's Israel (and God's church) in the world as HIS-story, a triumphant one.

For Reflection
- Write your life story and relate it to Christ's bringing you out of bondage. From your memory, what experiences have helped you learn of his love, grace, and power?

Prayer
Lord God, we exult in you. We praise you for your powerful yet subtle entrance into history, your revealing yourself as a redeemer of the helpless and oppressed, your bearing your people through all circumstances, bringing victory over sin and death. This is our story, too. We look forward to the day when all peoples shall behold your glory forever. Amen.

69
Save Me, O God, For The Waters Have Come Up To My Neck

I sink in deep mire,
*   where there is no foothold ...*
It is for your sake that I have borne reproach ...
It is zeal for your house that has consumed me ...
Insults have broken my heart ...
I looked for pity, but there was none;
*   for comforters, but I found none ...*
and for my thirst they gave me vinegar to drink.
— **Psalm 69:2, 7a, 9a, 20, 21b**

Theme: Lament and prayer for deliverance from persecution

Outline
1-18   As for me
    1-6   Rescue me from deadly foes.
    7-12   For your sake I am being persecuted.
    13-18   Help soon, Lord!
19-28   As for my persecutors
    19-21   You know their cruelty.
    22-28   Give them the judgment they deserve.
29-36   As for God
    29-36   I will hope in him and praise him.

Notes
- Imprecatory — Messianic Suffering
- Next to Psalm 22 this is the most quoted psalm in the New Testament.
- It is prophetic of Christ's sufferings. The reproaches and persecutions the prophets endured were a foreshadowing of the experience of the Christ, the true Servant of the Lord.
- Verse 35 suggests the time of the exile (long after David), and the language, ideas, and circumstances are much like Jeremiah's. (See Jeremiah 11:18 ff; 12:1 ff; 15:10 ff; 22:12 ff.)
- See Introduction on the Cursings or Imprecatory Psalms.

For Reflection
- What features of the sufferings of the psalmist point to the sufferings of Christ?
- Instead of the psalmist's curses, how did our Lord pray? (See Luke 22:42; 23:34; Matthew 5:44; Acts 7:60.)

Prayer
O God, your Son was hated without cause, insulted and ridiculed, bearing reproach for your sake. These were some of the signs of the depths of his love for you and for us all. May the Spirit prompt us to think upon his self-giving unto death and to respond with grateful hearts, renouncing sin and being renewed as faithful followers of our Lord Jesus Christ. Amen.

70
Be Pleased, O God, To Deliver me

O LORD, make haste to help me! ...
Let those be turned back
and brought to dishonor
who desire to hurt me ...
Let those who love your salvation
say evermore, "God is great!"
But I am poor and needy;
hasten to help me, O God!

— **Psalm 70:1b, 2b, 4b, 5a**

Theme: I am poor and needy

Outline
1	Come to my rescue quickly!
2-3	Let those seeking my life be shamed.
4	Let all who love your salvation remember how great you are!
5	Poor and needy, I need help, now.

Notes
- Lament
- This psalm is almost identical to Psalm 40:13-17.

For Reflection
- The psalmist knows enough of God as Savior to be glad and to encourage praise. At the same time he confesses to be poor and needy and in an urgent situation.
- When we meet difficult times, it is hard to say of God, "How great thou art!" But faith is not the same as feelings or moods. In times of difficulty, faith is a decision of the heart.

Prayer
Many are the afflictions, O God, that you permit us to endure. But with the psalmist we praise you and know that nothing shall separate us from your redeeming love and covenant faithfulness in Jesus Christ, your Son, our Lord. Amen.

71
In You, O Lord, I Take Refuge

Upon you I have leaned from my birth ...
   it was you who took me from my mother's womb ...
O God, from my youth you have taught me,
   and I still proclaim your wondrous deeds.
So even to old age and gray hairs,
   O God, do not forsake me,
until I proclaim your might
   to all the generations to come ...
You who have made me see many troubles
   and calamities will revive me again;
from the depths of the earth
   you will bring me up again.
                           — Psalm 71:6a, 17-18a, 20

Theme: Growing old gracefully

Outline

A prayer in three movements

1-8   Rescue me from the wicked, for I have leaned on you from birth, and I praise you for bringing me thus far safely.

9-16   Now that I'm getting old and facing more troubles, do not forsake me. I will always praise you for your mighty deeds.

17-24 Stay with me all the way, for I have lots of service to give you yet. Even in death — comfort me again.

Notes

- Lament
- The prayer's threefold movement reminds us of Jesus' prayer in three "waves" in Gethsemane and of Saint Paul's threefold prayer in 2 Corinthians 12:7-10.
- Written by one who has lived a long life of grace, but who is having a bad time of it of late. He wants the best gift of God that he may tell everyone of God's great deeds of salvation.
- "Depths of the earth" is where Sheol was thought to be located (v. 20). Even in death God can revive him!
- Verses 1-3 are identical to Psalm 31:1-3.

For Reflection
- Can I say about God what the psalmist says of him? (vv. 3, 5, 7, 15, 20-21).
- Use the psalm to tell those things to the Lord in your prayer.
- Are we in some way "telling" others of God's grace and power?

Prayer
Lord God, your love has been with me all my life, bringing me to faith, teaching me to rejoice in your mighty acts in Christ for our salvation. Enable me to face old age and death with a trust in you, a joy in serving you, and a grateful anticipation of the resurrection through Jesus Christ our Lord. Amen.

72
Give The King Your Justice, O God

May he judge your people with righteousness,
  and your poor with justice ...
May he defend the cause of the poor of the people,
  give deliverance to the needy,
  and crush the oppressor.
May he have dominion from sea to sea,
  and from the River to the ends of the earth ...
May all nations be blessed in him ...
Blessed be the LORD, the God of Israel,
  who alone does wondrous things.
  — Psalm 72:2, 4, 8, 17-18

Theme: Prayer for the king — the perfect king!

Outline

1-7 Prayer for God to give the king the gifts needed for him to rule with justice and righteousness.

8-14 Prayer he may have worldwide dominion, all nations serving him willingly.

15-17 Prayer that Israel's hopes and dreams will be fulfilled through his reign.

18-20 Doxology for ending of Book Two.

Notes
- Royal Messianic
- Probably composed by Solomon (remembering the prophecy about his father, David, [1 Kings 2:1-4]) as a prayer for his people to use on his (and their) behalf.
- Its vision of the future is not mere nationalism; it sees fulfillment for the nations as coming under the good and gracious rule and reign of God "who alone does wondrous things."
- God alone can make a ruler a good leader causing righteousness to flourish.
- As in our hymnals, this hymn for the ruler comes at the end of Book Two.
- "Amen" = True! It shall be so!

For Reflection
- While we dare not ever give messianic significance or claims to any current ruler, we can pray some of the petitions of this psalm. Which ones?

Prayer
Only you, Lord God, can make leaders truly good, and therefore we pray for your gifts to those who try to govern us, that justice and the redressing of human wrongs may flourish, and also the furthering of things that make for peace and plenty for all the world. The kingdom is yours, O God, and you have given all authority in heaven and on earth to your Son, Jesus Christ, our ascended Lord. Amen.

Book Three
Psalms 73 through 89

73
Truly God Is Good To The Upright

When my soul was embittered,
*   when I was pricked in heart,*
I was stupid and ignorant; ...
Nevertheless I am continually with you;
*   you hold my right hand.*
You guide me with your counsel,
*   and afterward you will receive me with honor.*
Whom have I in heaven but you?
*   And there is nothing on earth*
*   that I desire other than you.*
My flesh and my heart may fail;
*   but God is the strength of my heart*
*   and my portion forever.*
                            — **Psalm 73:21-26**

Theme: Faith sorely tried but triumphant

Outline

1-14   Seeing the wicked go on prospering offends our faith. People are swayed by it, and our efforts for God seem wasted!

15-20 If I had talked this way to others, I would betray my fellow believers. I know God will bring an end to them and their sinful ways.

21-28 Fellowship with God is the highest bliss one can know. All I know of my future is that I want to be with God. I trust him for it. Living with God is good, and I don't want it to ever end.

Notes
- Wisdom Poetry
- This and eleven other psalms are attributed to Asaph (one of David's musicians, a Levite), or to members of his family or guild, "the sons of Asaph." (See 1 Chronicles 6:31 ff.)
- This psalm begins Book Three in which God as judge and shepherd of his people is emphasized.

For Reflection
- This is one of the most marvelous psalms of all. It teaches us to be honest and open to God in our praying, to tell him our doubts and difficulties with his word and his ways. Notice how the psalmist spells out his complaint to God, and how he came to see the error of this thinking. Notice his restraint in airing his complaints about God to others (v. 15). What he realized was where his real bliss and his true riches lay.
- Note the sin of the godless — egotism and arrogance, while the godly learn the lighthearted freedom of humility.

Prayer
Teach us, Lord, by the example of the psalmist, and by the example of our Lord Jesus, who though troubled at the prospect of the cross, faithfully endured suffering and death and is raised and exalted with you and the Holy Spirit, ever one God. How you humble yourself, O God! Share that divine nature with us, that we may enjoy you forever. Amen.

74
O God, Why Do You Cast Us Off Forever?

O God, why do you cast us off forever?
Remember your congregation,
  which you acquired long ago ...
Remember Mount Zion, where you came to dwell ...
  the enemy has destroyed everything in the sanctuary ...
they desecrated the dwelling place of your name,
  bringing it to the ground ...
Rise up, O God, plead your cause;
  remember how the impious scoff at you all day long.
           — **Psalm 74:1a, 2, 3b, 7b, 22**

Theme: Lament on the destruction of the temple

Outline

1-3   Have you forgotten us? Look at your sanctuary!
4-9   The temple has been destroyed, desecrated.
10-11 Why don't you act?
12-17 You have the power (remember Exodus?).
18-23 Remember your covenant and your people. Don't let the impious keep scoffing at you!

Notes
- Lament
- For what happened, read 2 Kings 25:8-12. Babylonians totally destroyed the temple and led citizens into exile.
- Note the description of what the enemy did, not only in Jerusalem, but in the whole land (vv. 4-9, 18, 20).

For Reflection
- The psalmist is experiencing horrible shock. All that supported his faith in God was taken away — Mount Zion's temple with all its activity, his beloved city, and the ordered life he was accustomed to. During times when we are offended with God's apparent inaction in the face of infamy, do we restrain from expressing it out of loyal concern for the faith of others? Can we still tell God our feelings?

- The psalmist pleads with God. What are the pleas he makes and the reasons why God should do something? How do you plead with God in your prayers?
- Note the clues of a resilient faith the Spirit is bringing forth as he voices his lament.
- Prayer about God's word becomes a dialogue with the Holy Spirit.

Prayer
Lord God, when all the usual supports and props of our faith are taken away, we will remember the cross of Jesus and his shed blood, which sealed the covenant of our salvation. Make us emblems of your love and promises, that others may become part of your true dwelling-place and temple, people in whom you live and lead with your Spirit through Jesus Christ our Lord. Amen.

75
We Give Thanks To You, O God

"At the set time that I appoint
  I will judge with equity.
When the earth totters, with all its inhabitants,
  it is I who keep its pillars steady ..."
it is God who executes judgment,
  putting down one and lifting up another ...
But I will rejoice forever.
                              — Psalm 75:2-3, 7, 9a

Theme: Rejoice — God is in charge!

Outline
1	Thanks to God — for his nearness (in recent show of power on Israel's behalf).
2-3	God reassures his people, "I am in charge."
4-5	Warning to Israel's enemies against boasting.
6-8	God is the universal judge; wickedness brings his wrath.
9-10	Praise God — the wicked will be destroyed, and the righteous honored.

Notes
- Thanksgiving
- "Do not lift up your horns" = flaunt your strength like animals do (v. 4).
- "Insolent neck" = haughty attitude (v. 5).

For Reflection
- If God has ultimate responsibility for the world and will see that his purpose for creation will prevail, no one can avoid it or thwart it. Do we need to carry the world on our shoulders? Instead, can we with the psalmist rejoice that our Lord is King of kings and give our attention to telling his wondrous deeds and love in our life and words?

Prayer
Save us from our sinful pride and a haughty attitude. Give us the joy of forgiveness, the mind of Christ, and confidence in the victorious judgment of God over sin, death, and the devil, accomplished by the suffering and death of your Son. Lift us to resurrection life with him, Jesus Christ our Lord. Amen.

76
In Judah God Is Known, His Name Is Great In Israel

His abode has been established in Salem,
  his dwelling place in Zion.
There he broke the flashing arrows,
  the shield, the sword, and the weapons of war ...
Who can stand before you
  when once your anger is roused? ...
— Psalm 76:2-3, 7b

Theme: The God of Israel is judge of all the earth

Outline
1-3 The God of Israel has again shown his power, saving Jerusalem.
4-6 See the defeat of the enemy!
7-9 No one can withstand God's judgment.
10-12 Man's opposition serves only to advance God's glory.

Notes
- Praise
- Judah and Israel are synonyms (v. 1).
  Salem (short form of Shalom) is a short name of Jerusalem (v. 2), and Zion is the temple-mount. Shalom (peace) is the peace of God with new life and ultimate redemption for all the earth.
- Background for this psalm is the Assyrian ruler's siege of Jerusalem and his (Sennacherib's) mysterious defeat and retreat at God's hands. Told in Isaiah 36-37 (and in 2 Kings 18:12—26:19).

For Reflection
- "Human wrath serves only to praise you." God will use it toward the accomplishment of his purposes. Joseph said as much to his fearful brothers. (See Genesis 50:20; also Exodus 16; Romans 9:17; and Acts 2:23.)

Prayer
This is my Father's world;
Oh, let me not forget
That though the wrong seems oft so strong,
God is the ruler yet.

This is my Father's world;
Why should my heart be sad?
The Lord is king, let the heavens ring;
God reigns, let the earth be glad.

— Maltie Babcock, d. 1901

77
I Cry Aloud To God ...
That He May Hear Me

In the day of my trouble I seek the Lord ...
I am so troubled that I cannot speak ...
Will the Lord spurn forever,
and never again be favorable?
Has his steadfast love ceased forever?
Are his promises at an end for all time? ...
I will call to mind the deeds of the LORD;
I will remember your wonders of old ...
With your strong arm you redeemed your people.
— **Psalm 77:2a, 4b, 7-8, 11, 15a**

Theme: Prayer in deep crisis

Outline
1-10   The crisis
    1-3   I prayed but found no comfort.
    4-10   I began to think God has rejected us.
11-20   God's answer
    11-15   I meditated on the God who works wonders.
    16-20   How marvelous was his strong arm to redeem us!

Notes
- Lament
- With Jerusalem destroyed, much of Israel exiled, the psalmist asks tough questions only a strong faith can answer.
- His prayer is similar to that great prayer of the prophet Habakkuk (ch. 3), a contemporary.

For Reflection
- This psalm has a great lesson on prayer in crises. The psalmist pours out his feelings of despair to God, decides to remember and think about God's miraculous deeds and wondrous ways in Israel's past, and recalls the power God has, as seen in a great thunderstorm and in the experience of the exodus.
- This reveals to him God's character, and the result is a larger perspective on the crisis and a renewed hope. Clue: pour out

your heart, remember your Savior's love and work for you. See the larger picture God's word gives and in which comfort is to be found.

Prayer

Lord God, you are always near to hear our prayers in any crisis, and you are able to strengthen us in true faith in you in all circumstances. We thank you for your mighty works with Israel, and those mightiest works of all time, your Son's death for us all, your raising him from the dead that we might have life with you. Comfort us in life and in death through Jesus Christ our Lord. Amen.

78
Give Ear, O My People, To My Teaching

He established a decree in Jacob,
  and appointed a law in Israel,
which he commanded our ancestors
  to teach to their children;
that the next generation might know them ...
  so that they should set their hope in God,
and not forget the works of God,
  but keep his commandments.
How often they rebelled against him ...
  and grieved him.
— **Psalm 78:5-6a, 7, 40a**

Theme: God's goodness and Israel's recurring ingratitude

Outline
1-16 Do not be like our ancestors — stubborn, rebellious, and forgetful of God's mercies.
17-18 Refrain: They sinned and they tested God.
19-31 Even when God provided for them, they had to be punished.
32-39 They remembered God, but only briefly despite his mercies.
40-41 Refrain: Again they tested God.
42-55 God brought them into the promised land.
56-57 Refrain: They turned away faithless.
58-64 God deserted his dwelling at Shiloh and left them to their enemies.
65-72 He chose Judah and Mount Zion with David's line to shepherd his people.

Notes
- History — Salvation
- *Maskil* = parabolic pictures, teaching one can visualize and remember.
- For the "decree" of God or "testimony God established in Israel" (v. 5). (See Exodus 12:26-27; 13:8 ff; Deuteronomy 4:9; and 2 Timothy 2:2.)
- Two other psalms recite Israel's history: 105; 106.

- Israel's self-criticism is in stark contrast to the typical self-glorifying histories of nations. Israel's story is an account of human sin and failure and of God's undeserved but steadfast favor (grace).
- In his Bible, Dietrich Bonhoeffer wrote beside verses 8-9, "November 11, 1938 — Crystal Night," recalling the beginning of Nazi persecution of the Jews and the imprisoning of Christian pastors who protested.

For Reflection
- The psalm is full of theology. Jewish and Christian theology comes through stories of God's activity, revealing his character and purposes. God commands that his story be told and retold to the coming generation. (Doctrines or dogmas of faith are merely the synopsis of the great drama of God seeking and redeeming a lost humanity.)
- What light do verses 1-8 throw on the need for a family's reading the Bible (especially Bible stories)? If you make a list of God's mighty works, Israel's sins, and God's judgments, it can throw light on our sins and failures, and enable us to prize the wonderful covenant of grace and the gospel of Christ.

Prayer
Lord God, we will give ear to your teachings. Through the trials and testing of our journey, may your Spirit so strengthen us in your word, so that we and our children will anticipate joyfully the culminating revelation of your power, grace, and purpose for us, through Jesus Christ our Lord. Amen.

79
O God, The Nations Have Come Into Your Inheritance

O God, the nations have come into your inheritance,
   they have defiled your holy temple;
   they have laid Jerusalem in ruins ...
Help us, O God of our salvation,
   for the glory of your name
   deliver us, and forgive our sins,
   for your name's sake.
Why should the nations say,
   "Where is their God?"

— Psalm 79:1, 9-10a

Theme: Lament over the destruction of Jerusalem

Outline

1-4   Jerusalem is in ruins! The dead unburied; survivors are mocked!
5-7   Pour out your anger on the nations that don't know you.
8-13 Help us, forgive us, for your name's honor; we will ever thank you.

Notes
- Lament
- This is a prayer for vengeance and for justice: "Those heathen nations have got it coming, too!"
- This is a prayer for forgiveness and mercy.

For Reflection
- What are the reasons in verses 8-10 why the Lord should grant their prayer? God has permitted the worst to happen to the people of Jerusalem. What are the indications that the ones praying have not lost their faith?
- Will we still have faith in the Lord and pray if he permits destruction, sorrow, or tragedy to come our way?

Prayer
Though the fig tree does not blossom,
  and no fruit is on the vines;
though the produce of the olive fails
  and the fields yield no food;
though the flock is cut off from the fold
  and there is no herd in the stalls,
*yet I will rejoice in the L*ORD*;*
  I will exult in the God of my salvation.
— **Prayer of the prophet Habakkuk (3:17-18),**
a contemporary of the psalmist

80
Give Ear, O Shepherd Of Israel

Stir up your might
  and come to save us! ...
  look down from heaven, and see;
have regard for this vine,
  the stock that your right hand planted ...
Restore us, O LORD God of hosts;
  let your face shine, that we may be saved.
                    — **Psalm 80:2b, 14b-15, 19**

Theme: A prayer of Israel in exile

Outline
1-2   Show your power, shepherd of Israel.
3   Restore us.
4-6   How long must we be the scorn of our neighbors?
7   Restore us.
8-13   You planted the vine, and gave it growth. Why abandon it to foes?
14-18 Give us life and we will call on your name.
19   Restore us!

Notes
- Lament
- This psalm gives a theological interpretation of Israel's devastating experience — being overrun by the Babylonians and taken into exile. The figure of the vinedresser and the vine expresses the relation of God and Israel. (See Isaiah 5:1-7; Matthew 21:33-43.) God brought the vine from Egypt (Exodus), cleared the promised land (conquest), and planted it there, where it grew and flourished (reigns of David and Solomon). Now foreign armies ravage the land and Israel is scorned.
- "Restore us" "turn us again" suggests not merely return from exile, but make us "turned toward you again," a spiritual change, repentance, a daily renewal.

For Reflection
- Jesus used the vine figure to describe the relation of the Christian to him and to the Father. "I am the true vine and my Father is the vinedresser ... I am the vine, you are the branches ... Those who abide in me and I in them bear much fruit, because apart from me you can do nothing." (See John 15:1-11.)
- This is a symbolic picture of the church and a good prayer for it today.

Prayer
Lord God, you prune the vine that it may bear fruit. From the sufferings of Israel and the sufferings and death of Christ, you have brought forth our salvation with precious fruits of the Spirit for the blessing of all the earth. Keep us in the vine, abiding in Christ Jesus, that we may be vessels of your love, messengers of your love and grace to all the world. Amen.

81
Sing Aloud To God, Our Strength

Sing aloud to God our strength;
 shout for joy to the God of Jacob ...
Blow the trumpet at the new moon ...
 on our festal day ...
O that my people would listen to me,
 that Israel would walk in my ways! ...
I would feed you with the finest of the wheat,
 and with honey from the rock I would satisfy you.
— **Psalm 81:1, 3, 13, 16**

Theme: A word from God for the Feast of Booths

Outline

1-5 Call to celebrate the Feast of Booths (or tabernacles).
6-7 Remember the Lord's love and redeeming power in the exodus.
8-10 Be loyal to worship only Yahweh; no strange god.
11-12 Israel disobeyed in the past and got punished for it.
13-16 Despite Israel's failure, the way to God's blessing is open.

Notes
- Liturgy
- The Feast of Booths was one of the three great annual festivals at which all males of Israel were required to be present. They made booths of branches and leaves and dwelt in them during the festival to recall God's care for Israel during the wanderings in the wilderness without permanent houses. A joyful time. (See Deuteronomy 31:10; Leviticus 23:15-25.)

For Reflection
- Festivals are important for reinforcing and passing on the faith. In all of them we will get a glimpse into the heart of God and his purpose.
- The church's festivals should never become mere tradition. They need to be celebrated with the purpose of drawing near the Lord himself, relearning his redeeming ways and his will for us in our day.

- The festivals are calls: "O that my people would listen to me, that Israel would walk in my ways!"

Prayer
O God, you are our strength. May your Spirit enable us to celebrate your loving purpose in Christ for all human life that we and all people may feed on the Bread of Life, on "honey from the rock" for the satisfying nourishment of the hungry soul. Amen.

82
God Has Taken His Place In The Divine Council

God has taken his place in the divine council;
  in the midst of the gods he holds judgment:
"How long will you judge unjustly
  and show partiality to the wicked?
Give justice to the weak and the orphan;
  maintain the right of the lowly and the destitute.
Rescue the weak and the needy ..."
Rise up, O God, judge the earth;
  for all the nations belong to you!
— Psalm 82:1-4a, 8

Theme: Earthly rulers, God's delegates, are judged by him

Outline
1-4   Earthly rulers are rebuked for their injustice, and ordered to give justice to the weak, lowly, and destitute.
5-7   Unreformed, they shake foundations and, though "gods," they die for their misrule.
8   Prayer for God to govern the whole earth.

Notes
- Liturgy
- "The gods" = *Elohim*, the mighty ones, those with power, rulers or judges (v. 1). This interpretation was current in Jesus' day; he quoted the verse as referring to humans (not angels). (See John 10:34 ff.)

For Reflection
- Notice what God expects from his delegates, the rulers and powerful of earth (vv. 2-4).
- Notice what happens when they fail in these duties (v. 5).

Prayer
O heavenly Father, at whose hand the weak shall take no wrong nor the mighty escape just judgment; pour your grace upon

your servants our judges and magistrates, that by their true, fruitful and diligent execution of justice to all equally, you may be glorified, the commonwealth daily promoted, and we all live in peace and quietness, godliness and virtue; through Jesus Christ our Lord. Amen.

— Thomas Cranmer (1489-1556)
Archbishop of Canturbury,
editor-in-chief of the *Book of Common Prayer*

83
O God, Do Not Keep Silence

O God, do not keep silence;
do not hold your peace or be still, O God!
Even now your enemies ...
... lay crafty plans against your people ...
They say, "Come, let us wipe them out as a nation ..."
Let them know that you alone,
whose name is the Lord,
are the Most High over all the earth.
— **Psalm 83:1-2a, 3a, 4, 18**

Theme: Plea for God to defeat the enemy

Outline
1-4   Plea that God will not be still while enemies are closing in to destroy Israel.
5-8   We are threatened by a confederacy of surrounding nations.
9-12   Destroy them like you did the Midianites.
13-18   Overcome them, that they may acknowledge Yahweh as the most high over all the earth.

Notes
- Liturgy
- Their situation is like the one described in 2 Chronicles 20.
- The Midianite defeat by Gideon is told in Judges 7-8.

For Reflection
- Compare and contrast a New Testament prayer, when the Lord's followers faced frightening opposition. (See Acts 4:29-30.) What is the goal sought in the prayer? What are the means to it?

Prayer
Lord God, as we struggle in the conflict with evil and unbelief, keep before us the goal to be sought: not triumphalism but the redemption of all who are estranged from you and who need to hear the gospel. May your Holy Spirit encourage us to share with others humbly and gratefully the living Word of God, Jesus Christ our Lord. Amen.

84
How Lovely Is Your Dwelling Place

How lovely is your dwelling place,
*   O LORD of hosts!*
My soul longs, indeed it faints
*   for the courts of the LORD;*
my heart and flesh sing for joy
*   to the living God ...*
Happy are those who live in your house,
*   ever singing your praise ...*
*   in whose heart are the highways to Zion.*
*   — **Psalm 84:1-2, 4, 5b**

Theme: The happy worshiper

Outline

1-2	The psalmist longs for the house of God.
3-4	How happy are those who live there.
5-8	How happy those who go even through deserts in their pilgrimage to Zion.
9-12	How great a privilege to be close to the LORD, the source of all blessing.

Notes
- Praise — Zion
- Companion to Psalms 42 and 43 (also to 27; 61; 63).
- Valley of Baca, an arid place.
- From strength to strength — instead of fainting, they are refreshed.
- Verse 9 may be a reference to the king, or high priest, or the people.
- "Doorkeeper" = humblest servant.

For Reflection
- Look at verse 11b. Note the condition and the promise of a truly "abundant life" (John 10:10; 1 Corinthians 2:9-10), and the effect it had for some Christians (2 Corinthians 8:1-3, 7).

- When we read "your dwelling place, O Lord," we think of heaven. Saint Paul spoke of it as being "with the Lord." (See Philippians 1:23; 2 Corinthians 5:8; 1 Thessalonians 5:9-10.)
- "There have been times when I think we do not desire heaven, but more often I find myself wondering whether, in our heart of hearts, we have ever wanted anything else."[1]

Prayer
Dear heavenly Father, how surpassing great and good it is to live under you by faith, and in fellowship with you. Make us pilgrims to Zion to know our strength and renewal always comes from you, signs of the glorious things you have in store for those who love you, through Jesus Christ out Lord. Amen.

---

1. C. S. Lewis, *The Problem of Pain* (New York: Macmillan, 1962), p. 143.

85
Lord, You Were Favorable To Your Land

You forgave the iniquity of your people ...
you turned from your hot anger ...
Will you not revive us again,
so that your people may rejoice in you? ...
Steadfast love and faithfulness will meet;
righteousness and peace will kiss each other.
Faithfulness will spring up from the ground,
and righteousness will look down from the sky.
— **Psalm 85:2a, 3b, 6, 10-11**

Theme: Prayer for restoration of heart to God

Outline
1-3 You turned from your anger and forgave and restored your people.
4-7 Turn us to you, so we may rejoice in you.
8-13 The future is marvelous, your saving purpose accomplished.

Notes
- Liturgy — Prophetic
- Reflects the difficult time of returning from exile, dealing with disappointment and stirred by messianic hopes.

For Reflection
- Verses 8-13 are a prophetic promise and anticipation of the coming of Christ.
  a. Peace — Luke 2:14; Romans 5:1
  b. Salvation at hand — Matthew 1:21; Luke 2:30 ff
  c. Glory— Luke 2:32; John 1:14
  d. Steadfast love, truth, righteousness, peace — John 1:17; Romans 3:24-26
- The psalm is a beautiful prayer for the church today. Let's pray it for ourselves and all God's people.

Prayer
Lord God, at the birth of Jesus angels sang to our representatives, those poor shepherds, of peace on earth and glory to God. We praise you for his coming to us in our sore need, giving us forgiveness and salvation. Keep your church in the truth, rejoicing in you through your Son, Jesus Christ our Lord. Amen.

86
Incline Your Ear, O LORD, And Answer Me

Incline your ear, O LORD, and answer me,
  for I am poor and needy ...
Preserve my life, for I am devoted to you ...
There is none like you among the gods, O Lord,
  nor are there any works like yours.
All the nations you have made shall come
  and bow down before you, O Lord,
  and shall glorify your name.
Teach me your way, O LORD,
  that I may walk in your truth;
  give me an undivided heart to revere your name.
  — **Psalm 86:1-2a, 8-9, 11**

Theme: A personal prayer of devotion

Outline
1-7   Hear my prayer, for I am devoted to you.
8-13 When I think upon God, I am filled with gratitude and adoration.
14-17 Stand by me, Lord, and shame my enemies.

Notes
- Lament
- This is a collection of forty quotations from other sources (Psalms, Torah) for a personal prayer.
- This is the only psalm attributed to David in Book Three, and in view of Psalm 72:20, this could mean "like David's."
- A messianic prophecy of all nations turning to the Lord (v. 9).
- Verse 15 is word for word from Exodus 34:6, loosely quoted in other places in the Old Testament, a familiar expression.

For Reflection
- "Give me an undivided heart" — a remarkable and great prayer. Jesus said we could not serve two masters, only one (Luke 16:13). Soren Kierkegaard wrote, "Purity of heart is to will one thing"

and that is the good (God). Moses said it (Deuteronomy 6:4), Jeremiah spoke of the need for it (Jeremiah 32:39), as did James (James 4:8). Saint Paul gives us an example of it (Philippians 3:13-14).

Prayer
O Lord, let me not henceforth desire health or life, except to spend them for you, with you, and in you. You alone know what is good for me; do, therefore, what seems best to you. Give to me, or take from me; conform my will to yours; and grant that, with humble and perfect submission, and in holy confidence, I may receive the orders of your eternal Providence; and may equally adore all that comes to me from you; through Jesus Christ our Lord. Amen.

— **Blaise Pascal, 1623-1662**

87
On The Holy Mount
Stands The City He Founded

Glorious things are spoken of you,
  O city of God ...
Singers and dancers alike say,
  "All my springs are in you."
— **Psalm 87:3, 7**

Theme: Holy Zion to be mother of us all

Outline

1-3   Zion, City of God, founded by God and glorious.
4-6   God will reconcile old enemies to himself, and Zion will become Mother City to all the world.
7   Rejoicing for all its citizens.

Notes
- Praise — Zion
- For Zion, see note on Psalm 48. Other Psalms of Zion are 48 and 76.
- John Newton took the first line of the psalm for the theme of his hymn, "Glorious things of thee are spoken, Zion, city of our God." See notes for Psalm 48.
- "Springs" = fountains (v. 7).

For Reflection
- Like verse 9 in the preceding psalm, verses 4-6 are a messianic prophecy of all nations turning to Yahweh and becoming citizens of Zion. See Galatians 3:26-29 and 4:26, where Paul speaks of this reality. Paul regarded the church as being one, including the Israel of God in the Psalms and all the Old Testament. The church is heir to the promises and covenants and to all that God had given Israel. Israel continues to be the heir of God's promises (Romans 9:4-5; 11:1, 5-6).

Prayer
> *A multitude comes from the east and the west*
> *To sit at the feast of salvation*
> *With Abraham, Isaac, and Jacob, the blest,*
> *Obeying the Lord's invitation.*
>
> *O God, let us hear when our shepherd shall call*
> *In accents pervasive and tender,*
> *That while there is time we make haste, we and all,*
> *And find him, our mighty defender.*
> *Have mercy upon us, O Jesus!*
> — **Magnus Landstad, d. 1880**

88
O Lord, God Of My Salvation I Cry Out

Let my prayer come before you ...
For my soul is full of troubles,
*   and my life draws near to Sheol ...*
I am like ... those forsaken among the dead,
*   like the slain that lie in the grave,*
*   like those whom you remember no more ...*
Do you work wonders for the dead?
*   So the shades rise up to praise you ...*
O Lord, why do you cast me off?
— Psalm 88:2a, 3, 5, 10, 14a

Theme: From hopeless despair a cry to God

Outline

1-8   Hear my prayer. God, see my desperate situation.
9-12 When death comes, will I be beyond your love and care?
13-15 Why these terrors? I am calling on you!

Notes
- Lament
- This is the saddest psalm of all, a profound description of the tragedy of death.
- Sheol = abode of the dead, Shades = the dead (like shadows) (v. 3).
- The ancient fathers regarded this, like Psalm 22, to be the experience or utterance of Christ in his suffering. It is used on Maundy Thursday.

For Reflection
- To reach out to God in prayer while in such darkness, and getting no response but silence, is itself an eloquent expression of faith. (See Isaiah 50:10 and 1 John 1:5.)
- The psalmist expected only negative replies to his questions in verses 10-12. See the introductory section, "Life and Death in the Psalms." When and how did God answer these questions in the most surprising and amazing way? Read Luke 24:5-7, 44-

48. Also Luke 20:37-38. Make this a review of the stunning glory of the gospel by reading Hebrews 2:14-15; 1 Peter 1:3-5, 18-21; 2 Timothy 1:10; John 14:19; and 11:25-26.

Prayer
Lord God, your Son faced the darkness and death with us and for us, overcoming all the powers that stood against us. You raised and glorified him that we may have a complete redemption, forgiveness and life now and forever with you, Father, Son, and Holy Spirit. Blessed be God forever! Amen.

89
I Will Sing Of Your Steadfast Love, O Lord

I will sing of your steadfast love, O Lord, forever,
  with my mouth I will proclaim your faithfulness
    to all generations ...
You said, "I have made a covenant with my chosen one,
  I have sworn to my servant David:
'I will establish your descendants forever,
  and build your throne for all generations' " ...
But now you have spurned and rejected him;
  you are full of wrath against your anointed ...
How long, O Lord? Will you hide yourself forever?
              — **Psalm 89:1b, 3-4, 38, 46a**

Theme: God's promises and character are contradicted by circumstances

Outline

1-4   In his steadfast love and faithfulness, the Lord made a covenant with David that his seed and throne would be established forever.

5-18   Praise of the power and faithfulness of the Lord (expansion of vv. 1-2).

19-37   Elaboration of the covenant with David (expansion of vv. 3-4).

38-45   But now — look at our defeat and disgrace! What a contradiction to your word!

46-51   Plea for restoration soon (life is short and enemies insulting).

52   Book Three ends here.

Notes
- Royal Messianic
- This is a recital of messianic promises to David
- It was written during the exile. (See Jeremiah 33:19-26.)
- "Steadfast love" and "faithfulness" are spoken of seven times (attributes of the God of the covenant).

For Reflection
- Which of these verses (vv. 38-45) can be said of the Son of David who hung upon the cross on Calvary?
- Faith sings God's praise amid perplexity, defeat, and grief (v. 1). Israel had been overthrown by the Babylonians and the people taken away to exile.
- Why did God let that happen? The faithful struggled to reconcile their wretched situation with the promises and hope God had given them.
- When all the props we have relied on for our faith are taken from us, the future looks bleak, and we still hold fast to God — then faith is at its strongest and best. In the light of subsequent holy history, was this faith justified?

Prayer
Lord God, you were faithful to your word and to your covenant with David. Your beloved Son, descended of David, was anointed by you, crowned and enthroned upon a cross, and exalted in resurrection to be King of kings and Lord of lords, Savior of all. May your steadfast love of old and your faithfulness shine forth in our hearts and lives. Amen.

*Book Four
Psalms 90 through 106*

90
Lord, You Have Been Our Dwelling Place In All Generations

From everlasting to everlasting you are God.
You turn us back to dust,
  and say, "Turn back, you mortals" ...
For all our days pass away under your wrath;
  our years come to an end like a sigh ...
Turn, O Lord! How long?
  Have compassion on your servants!
Satisfy us in the morning with your steadfast love,
  so that we may rejoice and be glad all our days.
  — Psalm 90:2c-3, 9, 13-14

Theme: O God, our help in ages past

Outline

1-6	The eternal God is our home, and our brief lives are lived at his disposal.
7-12	God hates our sin — it has made our lives uncertain and difficult.
13-17	Prayer for God to restore us to his favor and give to us and to our children joy in the daily struggle.

Notes
- Lament
- Attributed to Moses. The author looks back on a long period of national existence (v. 1), is intensely aware of the brevity of human life and the seriousness of sin (for which they are suffering), and pleads for a brighter day. This suggests Israel is in the harsh discipline of exile rather than at the edge of the promised land.
- One of the greatest hymns is based on this psalm: Isaac Watts' "O God, Our Help In Ages Past."

For Reflection
- No one can escape the teaching of the seriousness of sin and its destructiveness. A conviction of our own sinful share in the human story can help us grasp the gospel and know its surprising

joy. Can we believe in grace without a realization of our sin? (See Romans 2:1-5; 3:20-26.)
- What are the three great requests of God in verses 14, 16, and 17?
- What is God's work? (See John 9:4; 17:4; 19:30; also Ephesians 2:10.)

Prayer
Lord God, make us sensible of the uncertainty and shortness of life, and of the seriousness of sin. Also show us every day your great love in the marvelous accomplishment of our redemption through Jesus Christ: crucified for us, risen for us, coming for us. Amen.

91
You Who Live In The Shelter Of The Most High

He will cover you with his pinions,
and under his wings you will find refuge ...
Because you have made the L ORD *your refuge,*
the Most High your dwelling place,
no evil shall befall you ...
For he will command his angels concerning you
to guard you in all your ways ...
Those who love me, I will deliver ...
I will be with them in trouble ...
and show them my salvation.
— **Psalm 91:4a, 9-10a, 11, 14a, 15b, 16b**

Theme: God's wonderful motherly love

Outline
1-2   Those who trust the L ORD will cling to him (like a bird under the mother hen's wings) for their security.
3-13 God's providential care described.
14-16 God's eightfold promise to those who love him.

Notes
- Affirmation of Faith

For Reflection
- This psalm must not be interpreted to mean that God will not let us experience danger, suffering, illness, or defeat, nor that, since God is taking care of us, we don't need to look after ourselves. The devil quoted verses 10-11 to Jesus in his temptation, but Jesus refused his suggestion. (See Matthew 4:5-7.)
- The list of fearful things (vv. 3-13) should be translated to our situation: auto accident, Alzheimer or cancer or psychiatric sections of the hospital, city muggers or rapists, killer viruses, divorce or bankruptcy court, people who are extremely hard to work with, and others.

- Considering "deliver" and "rescue" as synonyms, what are the seven other promises God makes to those who cleave to him in love and know his name? Can we let God be God and decide the how and the when of his delivering us?

Prayer
Lord God, make your fellowship so dear to us and so near that we know no greater comfort or protection. Enable us by your Holy Spirit to follow the example of your Son, resisting all temptations to security or success in anything but you and your loving purpose in Jesus Christ our Savior. Amen.

92
It Is Good To Give Thanks To The LORD

It is good to give thanks to the LORD,
to sing praises to your name, O Most High;
to declare your steadfast love in the morning,
and your faithfulness by night ...
For you, O LORD, have made me glad by your work.
— **Psalm 92:1-2, 4a**

Theme: A song for the sabbath day

Outline
1-3   How good it is to worship you with thanks and praise.
4-8   Good, because of your great works giving victory to the righteous.
9-15   Your enemies perish, but the righteous shall flourish.

Notes
- Thanksgiving
- "My horn" = (my strength), "poured oil" — as in a festival or anointed by priest when healed of sickness (v. 10).
- To understand this somewhat jarring verse think of VE Day 1945 (v. 11).
- Palm trees grow tall and provide fruit and building material (v. 12). Cedars of Lebanon can grow to be 120 feet tall.

For Reflection
- Verses 1-2 are good for beginning a morning's or evening's devotion.
- How can we share with the psalmist a heart made glad by the "great works of the Lord"? (v. 4). God's work is symbolized by a cross, his self-giving suffering with us and for us. This includes the whole story from the fall to the crucifixion and resurrection of Christ. To contemplate this humble self-giving of God for us is to open one's self to the "joy no one can take from you." (See John 16:22.)

Prayer

Lord God, how great are your works! The long patient preparation for Christ, his wondrous ministry, his death on the cross for us, his resurrection, and the sending of his Spirit to be with us — these mighty works all make us glad. Give us the joy to which we are called — growing in good works of faith, hope, and love, for we are your workmanship by your Spirit. Amen.

93
The LORD Is King

The LORD is king, he is robed in majesty ...
  your throne is established from of old,
  you are from everlasting ...
More majestic than the thunders of mighty waters,
  more majestic than the waves of the sea,
  majestic on high is the LORD.
                              — Psalm 93:1a, 2, 4

Theme: The majesty of Yahweh

Outline

1-2 Yahweh's eternal sovereignty is seen in the laws of the physical world.
3-4 The hostile powers of earth (like "floods"), however majestic or loud-sounding, threaten his rule in vain.
5   As established as the earth, so is your law and the holiness of your dwelling.

Notes
- Kingship of God/Enthronement
- An enthronement psalm (with 47; 96; 97; 98; 99) celebrating the kingship of Yahweh, the LORD.
- Floods of the Nile, the Euphrates, or "the Great Sea" were symbolic of the imperial powers threatening to overrun the world, as well as the power of evil generally.
- Decrees (*edah*) stand for the Torah (which includes such matters as creation, election, covenant, redemption, and the Commandments).

For Reflection
- Recall times when Israel experienced chaos, and through it all God continued to further his purpose, preserving Israel.
- Most of all, think of our king enthroned upon a cross, robed with a holy compassion, a glory revealing God's love, and of his rising the third day, showing God's majesty to be mightier than all the powers of evil.

Prayer

Lord God, how good it is for us to remember that your power and majesty are unchanging. When all the powers of evil opposed you, you triumphed over them by the gift of your Son, our redeemer. We see your glory in his resurrection and in your promise that nothing in life or death shall separate us from your enduring love in him — Christ Jesus our Lord. Amen.

94
O Lord, You God Of Vengeance ... Shine Forth!

Rise up, O judge of the earth ...
how long shall the wicked exult? ...
Happy are those whom you discipline, O Lord,
and whom you teach out of your law ...
If the Lord had not been my help,
my soul would soon have lived in the land of silence.
When I thought, "My foot is slipping,"
your steadfast love, O Lord, held me up.
When the cares of my heart are many,
your consolations cheer my soul.
— **Psalm 94:2a, 3b, 12, 17-19**

Theme: Yahweh is the just God of all the earth

Outline

1-3   Rise up, O Lord, and give the wicked what they deserve!
4-7   They crush your people, and you let them get away with it!
8-11 God replies: "You dull and foolish of heart: Of course, I see and hear. I even know your thoughts."
12-15 God disciplines his people but will never forsake them.
16-23 The Lord, having shown his love, will defend his people and put an end to evil.

Notes
- Lament
- Verses 12-13 are much needed counsel for everyone, especially when we feel powerless. "Blessed is the man you discipline ... that he might have patience when evil triumphs" (Bonhoeffer). The insights we receive from God's word and the fruits of the Spirit (as in Galatians 5:22-23) can "shine forth" in dark times, keeping us from defeat and despair and from self-righteousness and apathy. Instead of wanting recompense for the wicked, prayer for God to restrain and convert them is the New Testament way.

For Reflection
- "Who stands up for me against evildoers?" (v. 16). The psalmist says, "God!" When we think of the greed, indifference, and resultant cruelty of the powerful toward the poor of the world, the displaced, the immigrant (legal and illegal), the neglected and unloved children, the prisoner, and the gay person, as God's people we should stand up for their rights and their urgent needs (Proverbs 29:7).
- A beautiful confession of faith worthy of memorizing (vv. 17-19).

Prayer
Lord God, how blessed are those of your people who receive the discipline of your word and your Spirit, enabling them to share your heart for the world. Enable your church to share your heart toward the afflicted and to be your agents of mercy, faithfully witnessing of Christ and being cheered with a love no evil can destroy. So bless us, Father, Son, and Holy Spirit. Amen.

95
O Come, Let Us Sing To The LORD!

O come, let us sing to the LORD;
  let us make a joyful noise to the rock of our salvation!
Let us come into his presence with thanksgiving;
  let us make a joyful noise to him with songs of praise! ...
O that today you would hearken to his voice!
  Do not harden your hearts ...
                                    — **Psalm 95:1-2, 7c-8a**

Theme: The call to worship God

Outline
1-2   Let us come before God with songs of joyful adoration.
3-5   Think upon the greatness of him who created the world.
6   Let us worship with humility, submitting to his will.
7ab   For he has made us his people and shepherds us.
7c-11 God speaks: Do not harden your hearts and repeat the sins of your ancestors. Remember, and yield to me.

Notes
- Liturgy — Prophetic
- See Exodus 17:1-7 (or Numbers 20:1-13) for the account of Israel's rebellion or quarrel ("Meribah") with Moses and with God.
- This psalm has been used as an invitatory for daily use at the beginning of worship services (usually Matins) in both Western and Eastern churches. "Before the beginning of their prayers, Christians invite and exhort one another in words of this Psalm" (Athanasius — d. 373).
- For "today" see Hebrews 3:7—4:13 for its application.
- "Rest" meant first the promised land, but even more, the joy of living by trusting the covenant love and faithfulness of God to you.

For Reflection
- "To worship is to quicken the conscience by the holiness of God, to feed the mind with the truth of God, to purge his imagination by the beauty of God, to open the heart to the love of God, and

to devote the will to the purpose of God. All this is gathered up in that emotion which most cleanses us from selfishness because it is the most selfless of all emotions — adoration."[1]

Prayer

O God, Father, Son, and Holy Spirit, teach us to worship you. As we grow in faith, fill our hearts with adoration, that joyful emotion that gives rest to the soul, rest from self. Bring us to that perfect rest where, with all your people, we love and serve and enjoy you as you deserve. Amen.

---

1. William Temple, *Daily Readings from William Temple*, #13 (London: Hodder and Stoughton, 1951).

96
O Sing To The Lord A New Song

O sing to the Lord a new song;
sing to the Lord all the earth.
Sing to the Lord, bless his name;
tell of his salvation from day to day.
Declare his glory among the nations,
his marvelous works among all the peoples ...
Then shall all the trees of the forest sing for joy
before the Lord ...
for he is coming to judge the earth.
— **Psalm 96:1-3, 12b-13a**

Theme: Let the earth and all nations praise the Lord

Outline
1-3   Sing the praise of God and proclaim his glory among the nations.
4-6   The Lord alone is worthy of this, supreme above all.
7-9   All nations are called to come and behold his glory.
10-13 The Lord is king! All nature waits with anticipation of the joy of his righteous rule.

Notes
- Kingship of God/Enthronement
- A *new* song because of new beginnings for Israel, now back from exile, and the foretaste of new beginnings when God comes to govern all (v. 1). God as king and judge is welcomed, not feared!
- Enthronement psalms are eschatological, prophetic of the final goal when all nature participates in the joy of God's righteous rule. (See Romans 8:18-25.)
- "Holy splendor" — a variety of meanings and applications (v. 9).

For Reflection
- This is truly a missionary psalm, yearning on behalf of the most urgent need of the world for all the nations to come to Yahweh.

- Lovers of nature can rejoice that God's reign brings a new day for the "sea and all that fills it," the field "and everything in it" (including the little animals), and the trees of the forest.

Prayer
Lord Jesus, son of Mary, son of God, when you came to dwell among us, we saw the glory of the Father, the beauty of his truth and righteousness. Your marvelous works wrought for us a great salvation. May your Holy Spirit use us all in sharing the good news to all peoples everywhere; that they and all nature may rejoice with us under your blessed rule and reign. Glory to you, O God, Father, Son, and Holy Spirit. Amen.

97
The Lord Is King!
Let The Earth Rejoice

The Lord is king! Let the earth rejoice;
let the many coastlands be glad ...
The heavens proclaim his righteousness;
and all the peoples behold his glory.
Light dawns for the righteous,
and joy for the upright in heart.
— **Psalm 97:1, 6, 11**

Theme: The glory of God's reign

Outline
1-3   Rejoice, for Yahweh is king, powerful and righteous.
4-6   His manifestations to Israel (causing Nature to tremble) are known to all.
7-9   Idolators are shamed, but Israel rejoices at his exaltation.
10-12   Let Israel give thanks and obey.

Notes
- The Kingship of God/Enthronement
- "Coastlands" is a term for nations around the Mediterranean (v. 1). These people have cause to rejoice also at God's victory over his foes.
- "Your judgments" your ruling and overruling in history (and at history's end) (v. 8). Also the beautiful results of God's wonderful governing (in contrast to rebellious man's pathetic disorder).
- An eschatological hymn looking forward to a fulfillment to come.

For Reflection
- General characteristics the Lord loves in people: they hate evil because God does, they are faithful, they are righteous, and they are upright in heart. This is the kind of people God will make of us sinners, not a self-improvement piety. ("For we are his workmanship" — Ephesians 2:10.)
- Are we receptive to becoming this kind of person?

Prayer
We tremble along with nature at your awesome power and rejoice in your victorious overthrow of all evil. Forgive us our every failure to trust and obey, and cleanse and purify us for the glorious now-dawning light of your kingdom, where with your Son and the Holy Spirit you live and reign, now and forever. Amen.

98
O Sing To The LORD A New Song

O Sing to the LORD a new song,
for he has done marvelous things.
His right hand and his holy arm
have gotten him victory ...
Let the sea roar, and all that fills it,
the world and those who live in it.
Let the floods clap their hands,
let the hills sing together for joy
at the presence of the LORD,
for he is coming to judge the earth.

— Psalm 98:1, 7-9a

Theme: Exuberant praise for our victorious God

Outline
1-3   Praise the Lord for the redemption of Israel.
4-6   Let all the earth praise the true king, Yahweh.
7-9   Let all nature rejoice at his coming!

Notes
- Kingship of God/Enthronement
- This psalm expresses the gratitude and jubilation of Israel for its return from exile in Babylon.
- An eschatological hymn praising God for the coming redemption of the world (including people and planet).

For Reflection
- Notice the exuberant praise of God calling for nature to join in! There is a real kinship felt with nature under a common creator, having its proper good place in the coming redemption. This creates a respect and a will to be good stewards of the creation about us, something sadly forgotten by many Christians. Let us rejoice for nature's redemption at God's hands, too.
- "He has done marvelous things" (v. 1). To study the Old and New Testaments enables one to begin to see the marvels in the otherwise rugged and bloody story of Israel, and in the gift of Jesus Christ and the Spirit's work with the apostles. The marvel

is the grace, patience, and steadfast love of God and the glorious plans he has in store.
- It is sufficient reason to praise God every day, even on the worst days.

Prayer
Lord God, you are making all things new. Each song we sing of your praise is a new event, a foretaste of the glories to come, where, through the victorious death and resurrection of your beloved Son, we, with all nature, will jubilantly serve you in loving harmony forever. Amen.

99
The LORD Is King; Let The Peoples Tremble

The LORD is king; let the peoples tremble!
Mighty King, lover of justice ...
you have executed justice
and righteousness in Jacob
for the LORD our God is holy.
— Psalm 99:1a, 4, 9c

Theme: God is holy!

Outline

1-3a Yahweh is king in Zion and sovereign over all peoples.
3b   Holy is he!
4-5a He is a lover of justice, as Israel has experienced.
5b   Holy is he!
6-9a He both punishes and pardons (as Israel has experienced).
9b   The Lord our God is holy.

Notes

- Kingship of God/Enthronement (the last of the Enthronement Psalms)
- Holiness is an attribute of God, emphasizing his "wholly-otherness," separateness, inaccessibility, and awe-inspiring transcendence. (See Exodus 33:20; Isaiah 6:1-6.)
- Holiness is not something worked up, but a status conferred on a place, thing, time, or person in virtue of their nearness to God and their being used by God (such as holy ground, the Ark, vessels of the temple, festival, sabbaths, priests, people). (See Leviticus 11:44 and 20:26.) Its ethical character is conveyed in the idea of separateness, or "set-apartness," consecration or dedication.
- Priests are God's agents whose task was to ascertain the will of God (see 1 Samuel 23:6-12), to deliver instruction, to offer sacrifices, and to confer God's blessing. For Moses: Exodus 32:30 ff; Numbers 14:13 ff. For Aaron: Numbers 6:22 ff; 16:46. For Samuel: 1 Samuel 7:8-9; 12:16 ff.

For Reflection
- Voltaire thought the world was admirably arranged: God loved to forgive, and he loved to sin! Like many people today who forget what the psalmist could not forget from Israel's experience: forgiveness does not remove the discipline of punishment.
- Because God loves, he punishes as well as pardons. The punishment is discipline.
- God works for character in his people. (See Numbers 14:20-25; 2 Samuel 12:1-23; Exodus 20:5-6; Psalm 90.)

Prayer
Lord God, you love justice, you want righteousness for us, and you abhor our sins. Lead us to resemble you in heart and word and life, through your Son, Jesus Christ, who is our wisdom from you, our righteousness, and the one in whom we are consecrated and redeemed. Amen.

100
Make A Joyful Noise To The LORD

Worship the LORD with gladness;
  come into his presence with singing ...
Give thanks to him, bless his name.
For the LORD is good;
  his steadfast love endures forever,
  and his faithfulness to all generations.
— Psalm 100:2, 4b-5

Theme: All people are called to praise God

Outline

1-2   (As worshipers approach the temple gate, they turn toward the surrounding nations and proclaim): Worship Yahweh with glad shouts and singing.
3   (then facing each other they say) We are the people of the one true God and he cares for us.
4-5   (bidden to enter and worship) Thanks, praise to him who is forever good, loving, and faithful.

Notes
- Praise
- A mission psalm wanting all humanity to enjoy the living God with Israel.
- Used in daily synagogue service, where a familiar ancient refrain was used "his faithful love is everlasting."
- The poetic version of this psalm ending with the familiar doxology was written by William Kethe, friend of John Knox. It was put to music by Louis Bourgeois, OLD HUNDRED, and considered by Sir Arthur Sullivan to be "the greatest tune ever written."

For Reflection
- Is not verse 5 a joyful confession of faith, an abiding comfort and hope, a call to life-long praise of God?
- In a circular letter to his students, noting that many had died, Bonhoeffer wrote of this psalm "to awaken you to the right kind of joy in serious times." He says the joy belongs to this life; it is

not something worked up or demanded but it comes from God through "the poverty of the manger and the suffering of the cross." He suggests we look on him who is no stranger to any human suffering or sin and who accomplishes our redemption. This keeps us from becoming both insensitive to suffering from resignation to it.[1]

Prayer
Lord God, may peoples everywhere experience with us the joy of the Lord. You alone are good, and your steadfast love and faithfulness is revealed to us in Jesus Christ. Grant that we, in good days and bad, may ever look on him and praise you with joy. Amen.

---

1. Dietrich Bonhoeffer, *Meditations On The Psalms*, ed. by Edwin Robinson (Grand Rapids, Michigan: Zondervan, 2002).

101
I Will Sing Of Loyalty And Of Justice

I will study the way that is blameless.
When shall I attain it? ...
Morning by morning I will destroy
all the wicked in the land,
cutting off all evildoers
from the city of the Lord.

— Psalm 101:2, 8

Theme: David's mirror for rulers

Outline

1-2 God's covenant loyalty and justice, and my loyal response to it, is my intention.
3-4 As for me, I resolve:
    a. integrity in my palace and family,
    b. no time for anything base,
    c. no encouragement for those who fall away, and
    d. no tolerating evil.
5-8 As for my rule (government):
    a. the faithful will be encouraged,
    b. no tolerating of slander,
    c. or snobbery or class distinctions,
    d. loyal cooperation is to be expected from all,
    e. no deceitful practices or dishonesty, and
    f. court sessions (mornings) will be used to cut off evildoers from the land.

Notes
- Royal Messianic
- If written by David, it reveals his anxious concern of being worthy of God's trust and presence, especially after the terrifying lesson of Uzzah's death, a lesson in the holiness of God. (See 1 Samuel 6.) Loyalty to God, uprightness and integrity, is what God seeks through the covenant (Micah 6:8).

For Reflection
- Luther wrote an exposition of the psalm as a manual for the Christian prince — 78 pages! Some European princes felt it was written for them. It spells out the standard of integrity for those governing a nation, and for those governed. Its foundation is the loyalty and justice of God.
- How can we help to preserve the Christian faith from becoming mere civil religion?
- Will the state ever become anything but a temporary and wretched make-shift substitute for the kingdom of God? Jesus said, "My kingdom is not of this world" (John 18:36).

Prayer
Lord God, how have the mighty fallen from you and your justice in our day! Restore among us a new respect for honesty, faithfulness, and justice in our homes and in our governments. Grant renewal to your church, that it may proclaim your redeeming purpose and power and be exhibits of integrity. Amen.

102
Hear My Prayer, O Lord

My heart is stricken and withered like grass;
I am too wasted to eat my bread ...
I am like a lonely bird on the housetop ...
for you have lifted me up and thrown me aside ...
But you, O Lord, are enthroned forever ...
You will rise up and have compassion on Zion,
for it is time to favor it,
the appointed time has come.
— **Psalm 102:4, 7b, 10b, 12a, 13**

Theme: A prayer of one afflicted, faint, and pleading before the Lord

Outline
1-2 God, hear my cry of distress and answer soon!
3-11 I am suffering loneliness, ridicule, and sickness — because you are chastising me.
12-22 It's time for you, enthroned forever, to come and restore precious Zion that the we may proclaim you to all nations.
23-28 To return to my cry: I take hope for longer life and for a restored Zion in you, the eternal and changeless one.

Notes
- Penitential
- This is one of the seven penitential psalms (6; 32; 38; 51; 130; 143)
- Written by an exile during its last years, longing for home.

For Reflection
- Luther writes: "This is a psalm of prayer in which the ancient fathers — tired of the law, of sinning, and of dying — sigh from their very hearts and cry for the kingdom of grace promised to us in Christ."[1]
- Notice the contrast of the picture language in verses 1-11 (the exile's and Zion's sad condition) with that of verses 12-23 (faith's vision of a restored Zion). Saint Paul kept both the sorrows of

the present and the joys of the future in his perspective. (See 2 Corinthians 4:8-9, 18; 2 Corinthians 5:1-9.) What do we lose when we ignore or overlook either?

Prayer
Dear Lord Jesus, when we feel forsaken and thrown aside, may your Holy Spirit remind us that you know and share our sorrows and sickness, our loneliness and our death. Give us amidst our trials the bracing good cheer that our redemption is accomplished, our sin is covered, and that the Father waits for us with open arms and a jubilant resurrection homecoming where you with the Father and the Spirit live and reign now and forever. Amen.

---

1. Paul Althaus, *The Theology of Martin Luther* (Philadelphia: Fortress Press, 1966), p. 98.

103
Bless The LORD, O My Soul

Bless the LORD, O my soul,
  and all that is within me,
  bless his holy name.
Bless the LORD, O my soul,
  and do not forget all his benefits —
who forgives all your iniquity,
  who heals all your diseases,
who redeems your life from the Pit,
  who crowns you with steadfast love and mercy ...
  so great is his steadfast love toward those who fear him....
                    — **Psalm 103:1-4, 11b**

Theme: God's wondrous love for us

Outline

1-5   Praise to the LORD for our forgiveness, redemption, and his bountiful providence all the way.
6-10 He has dealt with Israel in mercy and grace.
11-14 God shows mercy and fatherly love for us.
15-18 Though we are frail and soon gone, he will be on hand to bless the faithful posterity.
19-22 A call to all creation to unite in one continued praise of him.

Notes
- Praise
- Aramaic aspects of the Hebrew text show it to have been written in its preserved form after the exile, but it is "like David."
- This psalm was inspiration for the hymn, "Praise, My Soul, The King Of Heaven," written by Henry F. Lyte in 1834.
- Soul = the life of the person with his faculties and powers.
- Bless = *barac*, applicable from God to man, and from man to God.
- Fear = to revere with profound respect and honor.
- Note the last phrase; when we pray this psalm we unite with a great company of angels, mighty ones, hosts, ministers, all his works....

For Reflection
- "All his benefits." List the five categories of benefits, thinking of the details of each one.
- The phrase, "those who fear him" (vv. 11, 13, 17), tells how we bless God: inwardly to revere him with respect, honor, tender feeling, and outwardly (v. 18), to keep his covenant and obey. In New Testament language, 1 John 3:23 sums it up.

Prayer
With all that is within us, we bless you, O Lord. For you bless us mortals with compassionate care and with redeeming love. We know this from one greater than Moses — your beloved Son, the Lamb who takes away the sin of the world and who has brought light and immortality to light, Jesus Christ, our Lord. Blessed be you, O God, Father, Son, and Holy Spirit. Amen.

104
Bless The LORD, O My Soul ... You Are Very Great

You stretch out the heavens like a tent ...
You set the earth on its foundations ...
You make springs gush forth in the valleys ...
You cause the grass to grow for the cattle,
*   and plants for people to use ...*
These all look to you,
*   to give them their food in due season;*
when you give to them, they gather it up;
*   when you open your hand,*
*   they are filled with good things.*
          — Psalm 104:2b, 5a, 10a, 14, 27-28

Theme: See God's greatness and goodness in nature

Outline

1-4   Creation reveals your incomparable majesty.
5-26   Your continued loving providential care is seen on earth, sea, and land, for all your creatures, and beautiful to see!
27-30   All life depends on you for sustenance.
31-35   I will praise you all my life, and may all that disturbs your joy in your work come to an end. Hallelujah!

Notes
- Praise — Creation
- A sequel to Psalm 103 (in which history reveals God). Psalm 104 shows that nature reveals God, too. These were written by the same writer.
- Last phrase, "Praise the LORD" in Hebrew is "Hallelujah," a word used only in the psalms, and appears here for the first time.

For Reflection
- "Love all God's creation, the whole and every grain of sand in it. Love every leaf, every ray of God's light. Love the animals, love the plants, love everything. If you love everything, you will perceive the divine mystery in things. Once you perceive it, you

will begin to comprehend it better every day. And you will come at last to love the whole world with an all-embracing love."[1]
- "Nature has some perfections, to show that she is in the image of God, and some defects, to show that she is only His image."[2]

Prayer

Lord God, teach us to love and care for your creation, because it is a reflection of your goodness. When this is hidden from us and we see threats and chaos, may your Holy Spirit show us your goodness and love better than all nature does — your Son, Jesus Christ, in whom is life eternal with you. May your Holy Spirit make him always near and dear to us. Amen.

---

1. Feodor Dostoevski, *The Brothers Karamazov* (London: Penguin Classics, 2003).

2. Blaise Pascal, *Pensees*, XXIV (London: Penguin Classics, 1995).

105
O Give Thanks To The Lord, Call On His Name

Make known his deeds among the peoples ...
Seek the Lord and his strength;
    seek his presence continually.
Remember the wonderful works he has done,
    his miracles, and the judgments he uttered ...
He is mindful of his covenant forever ...
So he brought his people out with joy ...
that they might keep his statutes
    and observe his laws.
Praise the Lord!
— **Psalm 105:1, 4-5, 8a, 43a, 45**

Theme: The wonder-filled early history of Israel

Outline
1-6	Proclaim and celebrate all that God has done.
7-11	He made a covenant with Abraham and never forgot it.
12-15	He protected a weak, wandering Israel.
16-22	He prepared ahead for them through Joseph.
23-25	He enabled them to multiply despite oppression.
26-36	He used Moses and Aaron for their release from Egypt.
37-45	He brought them into the promised land. Hallelujah!

Notes
- Praise — History
- This psalm, a thanksgiving for the faithfulness of God to his covenant, is a companion to Psalm 106 (a confession of Israel's faithlessness and disobedience).
- This is one of three psalms reciting Israel's holy history (78; 105; 106).

For Reflection
- Israel's story is mainly about God's activity, his "wonderful works" and faithfulness to his covenant promise.

- Note the ways God protects, delivers, trains, and provides for his people, ways that could not have been foreseen or predicted by human wisdom.
- What does this suggest for our faith in him today, confronted as we are by great threats?

Prayer
Lord God, in fulfillment of your promise to Abraham, you sent your Son, Jesus Christ, to us, and by his death and resurrection broke the enslaving power of evil, of sin and of death, freeing us for the promised land of living with you here by faith and in resurrection glory to come. Protect, provide, and train us through our pilgrimage by your word and your Holy Spirit. Amen.

106
Praise The LORD, O Give Thanks

Who can utter the mighty doings of the LORD,
   or declare all his praise? ...
Both we and our ancestors have sinned,
   we have committed iniquity, have done wickedly ...
Many times he delivered them
   but they were rebellious in their purposes,
   and were brought low through their iniquity.
Nevertheless he regarded their distress
   when he heard their cry.
For their sake, he remembered his covenant
   and showed compassion ... his steadfast love.
   — **Psalm 106:2, 6, 43-45**

Theme: A recital of Israel's sins and God's steadfast love

Outline

1-5	A call to praise and thank God for his steadfast love.
6-46	Time and again, Israel saw his goodness and saving power, yet failed to trust and obey him.
	7-12 At the Red Sea (Exodus 14:11-12).
	13-15 Craving meat at Rephidim (Exodus 17).
	16-18 Jealousy toward Moses and Aaron (Numbers 16:3-7).
	19-23 Golden calf (Exodus 32).
	24-27 Cowardly unbelief at the return of the spies (Numbers 13-14).
	28-31 Joined in Moabite worship (Numbers 20:1-13).
	32-33 Murmured at the waters of Meribah (Numbers 20:1-13).
	34-39 Sharing in Canaanite practices (Judges 2:1-5).
	40-46 A summary of Israel's cyclic experience of punishment, pardon, restoration, and relapse (Judges).
47	Concluding prayer for restoration.
48	Liturgical doxology (end of Book Four).

Notes
- Praise — History
- The last of three psalms of holy history (78; 105; 106).
- Appropriately begins with "Hallelujah," (meaning "Praise Yahweh" or "Praise the Lord"). The Greek spelling of the Hebrew word omitted the "h" at each end — "Alleluia."

For Reflection
- What is the benefit of knowing the history of Israel or of the Christian church?
- How can ignorance of it be a danger to spiritual life?

Prayer
O Gracious God, you suffer long and patiently, putting up with us sinners and making all things serve your purpose to save a lost humanity. We praise you for this abounding grace and pray we may become ever faithful and true to you, yielding in all things to your blessed rule and reign, through Jesus Christ our Lord. Amen.

Book Five
Psalms 107 through 150

Psalms 120-134 are a collection of fifteen songs used by pilgrims going up to Jerusalem for one of the three Covenant Festivals (Passover, Weeks, Booths). The title, "A Song Of Ascents" could be translated "a song for the way up." Jerusalem lies 2,300 feet above sea level.

107
O Give Thanks To The LORD, For He Is Good

O give thanks to the LORD, for he is good;
for his steadfast love endures forever.
Let the redeemed of the LORD say so,
those he redeemed from trouble ...
They cried to the LORD in their trouble,
and he delivered them from their distress ...
Let them thank the LORD for his steadfast love,
for his wonderful works to humankind.
— Psalm 107:1-2, 6, 8

Theme: God — deliverer in danger and calamity

Outline
1-3 Having returned from exile, let us thank the Lord.
4-42 Six pictures of God's saving love:
    4-9 travelers through the desert guided home,
    10-16 prisoners in dark dungeons released,
    17-22 sick (chastised for sin) made well,
    23-32 sailors in storm brought to port,
    33-38 a barren land is revived, and
    39-42 the needy and oppressed are defended.
43 Ponder these examples of God's love!

Notes
- Thanksgiving
- Book Five begins here.

For Reflection
- What good can come out of being brought so low that your resources are gone? The psalmist and Saint Paul would say, "That's when God shows his power." (See 2 Corinthians 1:9.)
- Everyone has experienced narrow escapes. How shall we interpret them? The world says, "Lucky you!" or thinks of the horoscope.
- The inspired psalmist tells us to see the redeeming love of God exemplified in them. Every healing is God's pushing back the hand of death. Every rescue is God's providential care.

- The purpose? That we may live with him, under his grace and leading and plan.
- But what about all the tragedies that do happen? Can we do better than to honestly leave them without explanation — and yet with faith?

Prayer
So bless us, O God, that when we are brought low, we may cherish your presence and know that you will show your loving care for us. No matter what happens, enable us to serve you at our station with growing faith, hope, and love through Jesus Christ our Lord. Amen.

108
My Heart Is Steadfast, O God

My heart is steadfast,
　I will sing and make melody.
　　Awake, my soul ...
Give victory with your right hand,
　and answer me,
　　so that those whom you love
　　may be rescued ...
O grant us help against the foe,
　for human help is worthless.
　　　　　　　　　　— Psalm 108:1, 6, 12

Theme: Praise and prayer for victory

Outline
1-5　　Praise of God (a repetition of Psalm 57:7-11).
6-13　Prayer for victory (a repetition of Psalm 60:6-12).

Notes
- Mixed — Lament
- An "editor" took portions of two older psalms and united them to make this new hymn for Israel in a new situation (similar to the older).
- The use of familiar words of praise followed by a familiar prayer for victory were brought together for a new use. (See Psalms 57 and 60.)

Prayer
Dear Lord, we thank you for the dependability and the good and faithful work of others, on whom we depend for many of your blessings. But only you can bring us through the trials and judgment our sins have brought upon us; only you can silence our foe.

　No strength of ours can match his might
　We would be lost, rejected.
　But now a champion comes to fight,
　Whom God himself elected.

Ask who this may be;
Lord of hosts is he!
Jesus Christ, our Lord,
God's only Son, adored.
He holds the field victorious.[1]

Keep us in Christ the victor and bring us to your eternal kingdom. Amen.

---

1. "A Mighty Fortress Is Our God," verse 2; words by Martin Luther (1483-1546).

109
Do Not Be Silent, O God Of My Praise

For wicked and deceitful mouths are opened against me ...
They beset me with words of hate ...
In return for my love they accuse me,
 even while I make prayer for them ...
But you, O LORD my Lord,
 act on my behalf for your name's sake;
 because your steadfast love is good, deliver me.
I am gone like a shadow at evening ...
Let them curse, but you will bless.
 Let my assailants be put to shame ...
— **Psalm 109:2a, 3a, 4, 21, 23a, 28**

Theme: An imprecatory psalm

Outline
1-5   Help me against my enemies who return evil for good.
6-19 Just listen to how my enemies curse me!
20-21 May the cruel things my enemies wish for me be turned on them!
22-25 I am almost gone. Save me. No matter how they curse, you bless — and this is what matters.

Notes
- Imprecatory
- According to one interpretation, the curses in verses 6-19 are the psalmist's on his enemy. If so, "Psalm 109 is as unabashed a hymn of hate as was ever written" (according to C. S. Lewis).
- The NRSV translators interpret it differently, the curses in verses 6-19 are known as a quotation, "They say...." The psalmist spells out to God all the venom of his enemy's curses, but resumes his more restrained plea for retribution in verses 20-25. In favor of this, note that the psalmist's enemies are plural, while the curses are for one person. The psalmist's curses (vv. 28-29) are mild in comparison and verse 20 can be translated, "This is the work of those who hate the Lord and speak evil against me."[1]
- Examples of the psalmists' cursings in other psalms are: 58:6-9; 59:11-13; 69:22-28; 137:8-9. (See Psalm Types, pp. 16-17.)

For Reflection
- We live in a different age. For the psalmist, retribution was evidence of God's sovereignty. For us, the Christ has come and taught us to do good to those who mistreat us, to pray for them (Matthew 5:43-45), and he exemplified this redemptive way of dealing with wrongs suffered.
- Peter writes: "Christ ... suffered for you, leaving you an example, so that you should follow in his steps ... When he was abused, he did not return abuse; when he suffered he did not threaten; but he entrusted himself to the one who judges justly" (1 Peter 2:21-23).

Prayer
Lord Jesus, as you were being nailed to the cross, you prayed for God to forgive your murderers and all who hate you. Dwell within us, that we may have the heart to bless those who curse us, to hate the evils done to us or others, and to pray for the Holy Spirit to restrain and convert them. Is this not your will for us? Amen.

---

1. Arnold Rhodes, *The Layman's Bible Commentary, Psalms* (Louisville: Westminster John Knox Press, 1962), p. 151.

110
The LORD Says To My Lord

The LORD says to my lord,
  "Sit at my right hand
until I make your enemies your footstool." ...
  Rule in the midst of your foes ...
  "You are a priest forever according to the order
    of Melchizedek."
                                    — Psalm 110:1, 2b, 4b

Theme: Messiah, king, and priest

Outline

1   Oracle I: Yahweh says to my Master, "Share my throne until I have overcome all your enemies."
2-3   At Zion, I empower you to rule fearlessly, even though surrounded by foes. Your people offer willing service in the freshness of youth.
4   Oracle II: By immutable decree you are a priest forever (like Melchizedek).
5-7   With God at your right, you will execute judgment over all nations, suffering won't stop your victory.

Notes
- Royal Messianic
- The same type as Psalms 2; 18; 20; 21; 45; 46; 72; 89; 132.
- The most quoted psalm in the New Testament. (See Acts 2:24 ff, Hebrews 1:5 ff.)
- Jesus speaks of it (Matthew 22:41 ff), assumes it was written by David and was an inspired oracle of God, referring to the Messiah-King, more than a mere descendant of David, or a warrior type. Therefore, Jesus' critics should not be scandalized by his claims. God's Messiah is different than earthly standards and perspectives would make him.

For Reflection
- Luther, concluding his 121-page exposition of the psalm, wrote: "This beautiful psalm, therefore, is the very core and quintessence of the whole Scripture. No other psalm prophesies as

abundantly and completely about Christ. It portrays the Lord and His entire kingdom and is full of comfort for Christians. For He is a lovable, comforting King and Priest for those poor, miserable, suffering, and plagued Christians on earth ... Therefore let Him be our dear King and Priest, who represents us before God forever."[1]

Prayer
Lord God, heavenly Father, how good and great it is to have Jesus Christ to be our king and priest forever. We have only one person to please, one all-sufficient priest, who takes away all sin and brings us to you in clothes of immortality and resurrection joy. Praise to you, O God, for your gift, too wonderful for words to express, and we offer ourselves to serve him in life and in death. Amen.

---

1. Martin Luther, *Luther's Works*, Vol. 1 (St. Louis: Concordia Publishing House, 1956), p. 348.

111
Praise The LORD!
I Will Give Thanks With My Whole Heart

Praise the LORD!
I will give thanks to the LORD with my whole heart,
  in the company of the upright, in the congregation.
Great are the works of the LORD,
  studied by all who delight in them.
— Psalm 111:1-2

Theme: The trustworthiness of Yahweh

Outline
1   Hallelujah! (praise Yahweh).
2-9   Praise him for the great revelation and redemption he has accomplished ("his works").
10   Wisdom comes through the fear of the LORD. Those who revere him practice it and gain more insight.

Notes
- Wisdom — Praise
- Both Psalm 111 and 112 are Acrostic or Alphabetical psalms; each of the 22 verses begins with a different letter of the Hebrew alphabet. Both were written by the same author and for use in worship.
- Works of God cited: Exodus, manna, covenant, Canaan, the law, redemption.

For Reflection
- A fitting Passover song, Luther thought Christians should pray it as a psalm of thanksgiving for the Lord's Supper, for the Passover was ultimately a sign and type of our Easter festival.
- What are the works of God for worshipers since Christ?
- How are they "studied by all who delight in them" today? The delight? Admiration, gratitude, awe, hope, confidence, and more.

Prayer
Lord God, great and marvelous are your works, bringing joy and hope to our hearts. Above all we praise you for your marvelous works through your beloved Son, Jesus our Lord. May the record of his life and ministry, his self-giving unto death on a cross, his resurrection, and his gift of your Holy Spirit, be for your church a source of delight and wonder, gratitude and praise. Amen.

112
Praise The LORD!
Happy Are Those Who Fear The LORD

Praise the LORD!
Happy are those who fear the LORD,
who greatly delight in his commandments.
Their descendants will be mighty in the land;
the generation of the upright will be blessed ...
The wicked see it and are angry ...
the desire of the wicked comes to nothing.
— **Psalm 112:1-2, 10**

Theme: The trustfulness of the godly person

Outline
1   How blest are those who fear the LORD.
2-9   The blessings and activities of these persons are cited.
10   The wicked look on it all with vexation and helpless rage.

Notes
- Wisdom
- See notes on companion Psalm 111.
- "This psalm was composed for the comfort of the pious over against the greed, temporal fame, and pleasure-madness of this earth; and thus it is to be used."[1]

For Reflection
- Luther says that reason cannot agree with the psalm, but "these are the words of the Spirit." "One must grasp them by faith ... not be guided by appearances but must take beginning and end together; then one will discover the truth of the prophet's statement: 'The righteous lack nothing, neither wealth nor fame nor pleasure; but the undertakings of the wicked shall not prosper.' "[2]

Prayer
Lord God, these words of your Spirit are true, though they may appear to contradict experience for a time. May your Spirit help us

not only to believe them, but to experience them as you see fit, for we want to learn obedience, led by the Spirit and the word of God. So bless your whole church, as we convey and interpret spiritual truths to those indwelt by the Spirit. Amen.

---

1. Martin Luther, "Selected Psalms," *Luther's Works*, Vol. 13 (St. Louis: Concordia Publishing House, 1956), p. 392.

2. *Ibid.*

113
Praise The LORD!
Praise, O Servants Of The LORD

Praise the LORD! ...
Who is like the LORD our God,
who is seated on high,
who looks far down
on the heavens and the earth?
He raises the poor from the dust
and lifts the needy from the ash heap.
— Psalm 113:1a, 5-7

Theme: God's transcendence and humility

Outline
1-3 Praise Yahweh, praise his name.
4-6 Exalted above heaven and earth, he yet humbles himself and "looks far down" into the whole creation.
7-9 For example, he lifts up the poor, and gives home and children to the barren woman.

Notes
- Praise
- One of the Hallel Psalms (113-118).
- First of the six psalms known in Judaism as "the Hallel" (or hymn of praise), four of them using the word "Hallelujah" (Praise ye Jah), a word occurring only in the psalms.
- This group of psalms were sung at the three great festivals of Passover, Tabernacles (or Booths), and Feast of Dedication (Hannukah). At Passover, Psalms 113-114 were sung before the meal and Psalms 115-118 after. (See Matthew 26:30 and Mark 14:26.)
- In verse 7 "the dust" and "ash heap" (or dunghill) where the poorest and outcasts sat to beg, are metaphors for extreme degradation and misery. This verse is from 1 Samuel 2:8 (Hannah's prayer) and the "barren woman" refers to Hannah's experience.
- The Hallelujah at the end of the verses could be the opening verse of Psalm 114 (as in Septuagint).

For Reflection
- "The mystery of God's condescension (better, his humility) in taking upon himself concern for the destitute, for barren Hannah and her like, is the unique and utterly amazing miracle throughout the Bible — the glory and self-emptying of God going hand in hand." (See Philippians 2:5-11 for the pattern.)
- "How much did God the Father humble himself when he not only formed a lump of clay, but also animated it with his breath. How much did God the Son humble himself: he became a man, he became the least among men, he took upon himself the form of a servant ... he became the unhappiest of men, he was made sin for us ... How much did God the Holy Spirit humble himself when he became a historian of the most particular, contemptible, and insignificant events on earth in order to reveal to man in his own language, in his own history, in his own ways the plans, the mysteries, and the ways of the Godhead?"[1]

Prayer
Lord Jesus, you left the glory of heaven to come and be one of us, that we might be raised from the dust to live with you and share your love. May your children ever speak of you with gratitude and adoring praise through Jesus Christ our Lord. Amen.

---

1. Johann Georg Hamann (1730-1788), from *London Schriften*, and quoted in *Pro Ecclesia*, Vol. XIV, No. 2, p. 212.

114
When Israel Went Out From Egypt

When Israel went out from Egypt ...
The sea looked and fled;
  Jordan turned back.
The mountains skipped like rams,
  the hills like lambs ...
Tremble, O earth, at the presence of the LORD.
— **Psalm 114:1a, 3-4, 7a**

Theme: Even nature was surprised!

Outline
1-2   In the exodus, God made Israel his dwelling and kingdom.
3-4   The Red Sea, Jordan River, and mountains obeyed, awestruck!
5-6   Nature is challenged to explain its behavior.
7-8   Tremble at God's presence and power to redeem!

Notes
- Praise — Salvation
- One of the Hallel Psalms (113-118).
- Exquisite poetry with vivid dramatic portrayal of God's presence in the exodus.
- Israel's exodus was a type of the greater deliverance from the bondage of sin by Christ's death and resurrection.

For Reflection
- Living in our man-centered society, how can a Christian share with the psalmist something of the awe and wonder he expresses at the supernatural power of God?
- This power is seen not only in the events of the exodus but the greater miracle of the resurrection of Christ.
- The miracles are inexplicable, but faith can believe they happened as scripture testifies.

Prayer
Lord God, in the experience of Israel and the coming of Christ, you showed your power to redeem and to renew us. May your Spirit give us confidence in your faithfulness and reverent awe of the power of your love, that we may bear a grateful witness to the world of your grace in Jesus Christ our Lord. Amen.

115
Not To Us, O Lord ...
But To Your Name Give Glory

Not to us, O Lord, not to us, but to your name give glory,
  for the sake of your steadfast love and your faithfulness.
Why should the nations say,
  "Where is their God?"
Our God is in the heavens;
  he does whatever he pleases.
Their idols are silver and gold,
  the work of human hands ...
O Israel, trust in the Lord! ...
The Lord has been mindful of us; he will bless us ...
  — **Psalm 115:1-4, 9a, 12a**

Theme: The power of the Lord and the impotence of idols

Outline

1-2   Show your great power and love, Lord; answer the mockery of neighboring peoples.
3-8   Our God does what he pleases. The heathen's idols are their own helpless handiwork.
9-13 We must trust the Lord and await his blessing.
14-18 Prayers for blessing, with resolve, "We will bless the Lord forevermore."

Notes
- Praise — Creation/History
- One of the Hallel Psalms (113-118).
- Probably written after the exile when, realizing their weakness, they know they must wait yet for a fulfillment to come.
- Ezra 3:10 tells how a psalm was used in worship with priests and Levites stationed to praise the Lord with trumpets, cymbals "according to the direction of King David ... sang responsively, praising and giving thanks to the Lord ... And all the people responded with a great shout...."
- Verses 1-8 can be chanted by Levite choir, verses 9-11 by a leader and choir responsively, and verses 12-18 by the Levite choir again.

253

- This psalm was identified by the Latin words, *Non nobis* ("Not to us"). Henry V "gathering his armie togither, gaue thanks to almightie God for so happie a victorie, causing his prelats and chapleins to sing this psalm ... and commanded euerie man to kneele downe on the ground at this verse: '*Non nobis*.' "[1]

For Reflection
- "Where is God?" has been the big question raised in response to the experience of the Holocaust and the violence in the twentieth century. Christians are challenged to answer. How did the psalmist respond in similar distress?
- "He does whatever he pleases." A wonderful statement reflecting faith in God's power and supremacy, his freedom from all manipulation by anyone, his pleasure in bringing about a great redemption. (See the phrase, "It pleased God ..." in Colossians 1:19; 1 Corinthians 1:21; and Galatians 1:16.)
- By contrast, idols, human ideologies and philosophies, and idolatrous devotions only make us cruel and would enslave us to fate or karma or Allah or drugs, sex, pleasure, greed, and the like. True faith in God issues in a training in righteous living. (See Micah 6:8 and Titus 2:11-14.) The psalmist resolved to trust the Lord and ends up praising him. This is an example for us.

Prayer
L̲o̲r̲d̲ God, how good it is to live under your steadfast love and faithfulness, instead of putting ourselves at the mercy of ideology or horoscope or fate or karma. You do what pleases you, and that is the loving gift to us of your best and dearest, your beloved Son, Jesus Christ, in whom you are well-pleased. May we enter humbly and gratefully and boldly into your good pleasure for us — his eternal living fellowship. Amen.

---

1. Quoted by A. F. Kirkpatrick in *The Book of Psalms* (Cambridge: Cambridge University Press, 1957), p. 683.

116
I Love The Lord, Because He Has Heard My Voice

When I was brought low, he saved me.
Return, O my soul, to your rest,
for the Lord has dealt bountifully with you.
For you have delivered my soul from death,
my eyes from tears,
my feet from stumbling ...
What shall I return to the Lord
for all his bounty to me?

— Psalm 116:6b-8, 12a

Theme: Exuberant thanks for recovery from illness

Outline

1-4 I love the Lord, who heard my prayer in my distress and gave me new life and hope.
5-11 Grateful meditation on this grace that was shown me.
12-19 What shall I render to the Lord? Public witness of my covenant loyalty by faithful worship with his people.

Notes
- Thanksgiving
- One of the Hallel Psalms (113-118).
- "Snares of death ... Sheol" (v. 3). Death like a hunter about to trap and seize his victim.
- "The simple" are those lacking intelligence or wisdom and experience and need God's special care to protect them (v. 6). (See Matthew 11:25.)
- "Return to your rest" (v. 7). According to Alan Richardson, rest has several meanings:
  a. an end to struggle (in this case to get well, the refreshment of normal healthy life again);
  b. peace, security;
  c. satisfaction in attaining the goal; no more fruitless labor;
  d. resting places, permanent dwellings (John 14:1); and
  e. salvation in Christ (Hebrews 3:7—4:11).[1]

- "Everyone is a liar" = lost all faith in man (v. 11).
- Cup, a thanksgiving ritual (v. 13). (See 1 Corinthians 10:16.)
- "Faithful ones" (v. 15). The Hebrew word is related to *chesed*, God's covenant love, his "steadfast love." Here the word stands for the one who is the object of that love, one drawn by God into covenant relationship.

For Reflection
- We all have the "snares of death" awaiting us with its "pangs." We all have feared it.
- Verse 15 reminds us our dying and death are not a matter of indifference to God. Rather, it is "precious" (dear to him, or costly) because it was thought to break off relationship with him. (See Psalm 6:5.)
- In the light of Christ's resurrection and the gospel, our death has been costly to God in bringing about our complete redemption.
- Jesus shared the snares and pangs of death for us and with us, so that in dying and death we are not alone. He is with us. Nothing shall separate us from the LORD (Romans 8:38-39).

Prayer

O eternal and most glorious God ... You who assure us that precious in your sight is the death of your saints, enable us in life and death, seriously to consider the value, the price of a soul. It is precious, O Lord, because your image is stamped and imprinted upon it; precious, because the blood of your Son was paid for it; precious, because your blessed Spirit, the Holy Ghost works upon it, and tests it, by his various fires; and precious, because it is entered into your revenue, and made a part of your treasure.

— **John Donne (1572-1631)**

---

1. Alan Richardson, *A Theological Wordbook of the Bible* (New York: Macmillan, 1951), p. 192.

117
Praise The LORD, All You Nations!

Praise the LORD, all you nations!
Extol him, all you peoples!
For great is his steadfast love toward us,
and the faithfulness of the LORD endures forever.
Praise the LORD!

— Psalm 117

Theme: A missionary psalm

Outline

1 A call to all nations and peoples to praise Yahweh.
2 The reason: his mighty love for us all and his faithfulness prevails forever! Therefore, praise him!

Notes
- Praise
- One of the Hallel Psalms (113-118).
- A call to all nations and peoples to join Israel in praising Yahweh, emphasizing the vocation of covenant people, God's missionaries to the whole world. (See Genesis 12:3 [to Abraham] "In you all the families of the earth shall be blessed." See also Isaiah 49:6; Galatians 3:8; Romans 15:8-12.)
- This is a truly messianic psalm. Luther believed that the whole book of Acts was written because of this psalm.
- This is the shortest psalm and chapter in the Bible, and like a gem, precious.
- Psalm 67 also shares this missionary vision.

For Reflection
- In 1530, Luther wrote a pamphlet expounding the message of this psalm. "This is a short, easy psalm, doubtless made this way so that everyone might pay more attention to it and remember better what is said." Luther sees in it four things:
  a. a prophecy of the gospel and the kingdom of Christ;
     "We heathen are assured that we, too, belong to God and in heaven ... even though we are not Abraham's flesh and blood."

   b. a revelation of the kingdom of Christ;

It is spiritual, heavenly, and eternal, "ruled without and above all laws, regulations, and outward means." In Ephesians 3:5, Saint Paul says it was revealed to the apostles that the heathen could be God's people without the Law of Moses.

   c. instruction; and

It teaches us the greatest wisdom on earth ... the wisdom of faith. It sings out: "God's steadfast love toward us prevails," for instance, God's grace "rules" over us, "more powerful in and over us than all anger, sin, and evil." Grace retains the upper hand and dominion.

   d. exhortation.

"Since of ourselves we are nothing but have everything from God, it is easy to see that we can give Him nothing; neither can we repay Him for His grace ... The only thing left, therefore, is for us to praise and thank Him ... Then out with it, and freely and openly confess this before the world — preach, praise, glorify, and give thanks!"[1]

- What could happen to a Christian's outlook and life if this psalm is prayed often? Is this important for the church in our day?

Prayer

Lord God, you called us to a great vocation, to be agents of your promised blessing to the whole world, witnesses to the surpassing great gift to all of your Son, Jesus Christ the Lord, and of your enduring grace for all. May your Holy Spirit cause us to hold dear your great love and faithfulness, and give us the humility and courage to fulfill our calling in Christ. Bless the whole world. Amen.

---

1. Martin Luther, *Luther's Works*, Vol. 14 (St. Louis: Concordia Publishing House, 1956), pp. 3-39.

118
O Give Thanks To The Lord, For He Is Good

There are glad songs of victory in the tents of the
righteous ...
I shall not die, but I shall live,
and recount the deeds of the Lord ...
The stone that the builders rejected
has become the chief cornerstone.
This is the Lord's doing;
it is marvelous in our eyes ...
Blessed is the one who comes in the name of the Lord.
— Psalm 118:15a, 17, 22-23, 26a

Theme: Jubilant celebration of Yahweh's covenant love

Outline
A Worship Service
1   A new convert and the congregation are welcomed by priests.
2-4   Priests, congregation, and convert gather at gates, and repeat a creed.
5-9   The new convert, coming to Jerusalem, having been taught, now tells his experience of God's covenant love.
10-14   Congregation (Israel) echoes his story (v. 14 — a chorus, from Exodus 15:2).
15-18   At the temple gates, priests and people give their testimony.
19-20   Worshipers request entrance; the priest invites them in.
21-25   Now in the holy place, there is thanks and praise to God by all as the marvelous salvation from the Lord is proclaimed.
26-29   Branches from the Feast of Booths are brought to the altar as a climax, with benediction, thanksgiving, and praise.

Notes
- Thanksgiving
- One of the Hallel Psalms (113-118).
- This psalm may have been first used at the Feast of Tabernacles (or Booths) in the time of Nehemiah. (See Nehemiah 8:14-18.)

- This was always sung at Passovers, the last of the Hallel (Psalms 113-118).
- "Cornerstone" (v. 22) = the top or crowning stone, "the head of the corner" bonding the walls and completing the building. Powers of the world rejected it, but God gave it the most important and honored place in his kingdom. Jesus applied the passage to himself (Matthew 21:42; Mark 12:10-11; Luke 20:17) and Peter quotes it (Acts 4:11; 1 Peter 2:7). (See also Ephesians 2:20.) Christ was Israel's real representative, who fulfilled the calling in which Israel had failed.
- "Hosanna" (vv. 25-26) — These were used by the disciples as Jesus rode into Jerusalem (Palm Sunday) to welcome him. "Save us, we pray" ("Hosanna") became a familiar shout of acclamation, and "he who comes" had become a reference to the Messiah (Matthew 11:3; John 4:25).
- "Horns of the altar" (v. 27) = the projections at its corners. Altars provided sanctuary for guilty fugitives, who, in a ritual act of "taking hold of the horns" were safe while awaiting trial. (See 1 Kings 2:28.) This is a symbol of God's mercy.
- This was Luther's favorite psalm. "Although the entire Psalter and all of the Holy Scripture are dear to me as my only comfort and source of life, I fell in love with this psalm, especially ... [it] proved a friend and helped me out of many great troubles ... This psalm praises God especially for the greatest benefit He bestowed on the world, namely, for Christ and His kingdom of grace."[1]

For Reflection
- This psalm is one of the propers for the day of Easter. What makes it so very appropriate in our celebration of "The Resurrection Of Our Lord"?
- Look for verses that can be prophetic hints of Christ's passion and resurrection.

Prayer
O God, you showed your glory in the obedience of Jesus unto death on a cross, your power in raising him from the dead, and your redeeming love by exalting him to be Lord of all. May all who profess faith in Jesus come to share his kind of love, which no evil

can destroy, so that all the world may be drawn to you, entering your kingdom through the gate, Jesus Christ our Lord. Amen.

---

1. Martin Luther, *Luther's Works*, Vol. 14 (St. Louis: Concordia Publishing House, 1956), pp. 45, 47.

119
Happy Are Those Whose Way Is Blameless

Happy are those ...
  who seek him with their whole heart ...
Open my eyes, so that I may behold
  wondrous things out of your law ...
My soul clings to the dust;
  revive me according to your word ...
Turn my eyes from looking at vanities;
  give me life in your ways ...
Your word is a lamp to my feet
  and a light to my path ...
Your decrees are my heritage forever;
  they are the joy of my heart.
                      — Psalm 119:2b, 18, 25, 37, 105, 116

Theme: The ABC's of the praise, power, love, and use of God's word

Notes
- Acrostic or Alphabetical
- This is the longest chapter in the Bible. Its 22 stanzas or strophes (each eight verses long) uses one of the 22 letters of the Hebrew alphabet. Each verse of each stanza begins with the same letter. This is carefully crafted so as to be easily memorized and recited.
- Its theme is not the commandments but the entire word of God. Law (Torah) came to be the word for "all divine revelation as the guide of life." It came to designate the first five books of our Bible (Genesis-Deuteronomy, the Pentateuch), with its teaching of sin and judgment, election, redemption, covenant and grace, God's creative purpose and redeeming, loving plan. (For Lutherans, this includes in embryo the law and the gospel.)
- Synonyms for "law": word, sayings, commandments, statutes, judgments, ordinances, precepts, testimony, ways, path.
- The author is "a man ravished by moral beauty" (C. S. Lewis). Who was he? One sorely tried, but he recognized God's loving discipline in his afflictions, and he suffered ill-treatment and contempt for his devotion to God: he was persecuted by powerful

wicked persons and also by faithless Israelites; he was in danger of his life at times; he got indignant; he felt sorrow; he was tempted by bad examples but resisted them, experienced humiliation. Who most fits this description? Jesus!

For Reflection
- In each stanza look for
  a. the purpose of God's word;
  b. what God's word has done for him (and can do for you);
  c. where God's word has led and taken him;
  d. his pressing need for the word; and
  e. the correction, the comfort, and the blessings of the word.
- God's word in the scriptures is spoken of as
  a. first and foremost, the Incarnate Word, Jesus (John 1:1-4);
  b. the recorded or written word (holy scripture), "the manger in which the Christ lays" (Luther), which exists to make Christ known and loved; and
  c. the proclaimed word of the apostles, preachers, teachers, and the faithful witnesses of the gospel of Christ and his grace.

Prayer
Lord God, we praise and thank you that you gather and guide your people through your word: the Incarnate Word that is Jesus, the written word that reveals him, and the spoken word that proclaims him. For Jesus' sake, may your Holy Spirit awaken our hearts to behold your glory that we may be led to faithfulness and enabled to love you with all our heart and our neighbor as ourselves, through Jesus Christ our Lord. Amen.

120
In My Distress I Cry To The LORD

Too long have I had my dwelling
among those who hate peace.
I am for peace;
but when I speak,
they are for war!

— Psalm 120:6-7

Theme: Living among the hostile

Outline

1-2   In distress, he prays for deliverance from false accusations, slander, and hypocrisy.

3-4   Appropriate retribution is coming from God for such wrongs!

5-8   The psalmist's situation — having to live among those who threaten by their hostility.

Notes
- Lament
- One of the Song of Ascents (Psalms 120-134).
- "Glowing coals of the broom tree" — used to produce very hot fires (v. 4).
- Meshach, Kedar refer to far-away barbarians, a way of describing fellow citizens nearby who are hostile and fiercely uncharitable. It may also refer to hostile people encountered by the pilgrims on their way to Passover in Jerusalem — the city of "salem" or shalom, peace (v. 5).

For Reflection
- What can a person do when falsely accused or threatened?
- The psalmist prayed, trusting God to protect him and bring retribution.
- What does Jesus tell us to do? (See Matthew 5:11-12.)
- When living among people who are hostile to our faith, see what Peter suggests in his epistle: 1 Peter 2:23; 3:9, 15-16.

Prayer
Lord Jesus, you have told us that in you we will have peace, and in the world, tribulation. Grant us the good cheer of your wondrous love for us that we may let this peace of God rule in our hearts and follow your example in all our conflicts and distress. Amen.

121
I Lift Up My Eyes To The Hills

The LORD will keep you from all evil;
*   he will keep your life.*
The LORD will keep
*   your going out and your coming in*
*   from this time on and forevermore.*
                                      — Psalm 121:7-8

Theme: The Lord is your guardian

Outline
1-2	My help comes not from hilltops (those high places where Baal and Astarte were worshiped), nor from Jerusalem (built on a hill). My help comes from the LORD himself!
3-4	Israel's watchman is never off duty.
5-6	The LORD is our protection from all dangers, especially the sun and the moon.
7-8	Our security in all our undertakings, all our comings and goings, is in the lands of the LORD, who will preserve us from evil forever.

Notes
- Affirmation of Faith
- One of the Song of Ascents (Psalms 120-134).
- The traveler's psalm — originally written for pilgrims en route to Jerusalem (2,300 feet above sea level) for a festival.
- Dangers and discomforts of travel are a concern of God: a foot slipping, sunstroke, or moonstroke (ancients thought its light could bring on madness or lunacy).
- It may have been used antiphonally: speaker A (vv. 1-2), speaker B (vv. 3-4), and the whole group responding (vv. 5-8).

For Reflection
- Are there any limits to God's ability to preserve his people from harm? (See Ephesians 3:20; Jude 24.) Our answer should conclude with Romans 8:31-39.

Prayer

Lord God, you have called your servants to ventures of which we cannot see the ending, by paths as yet untrodden, through perils unknown. Give us faith to go out with good courage, not knowing where we go, but only that your hand is leading us and your love supporting us; through Jesus Christ our Lord. Amen.

— from *Lutheran Book of Worship*, p. 153

122
I Was Glad When They Said To Me

I was glad when they said to me,
    "Let us go to the house of the Lord!" ...
Our feet are standing within your gates,
    O Jerusalem ...
Pray for the peace of Jerusalem ...
For the sake of my relatives and friends ...
For the sake of the house of the L<small>ORD</small> *our God,*
    I will seek your good.
                              — **Psalm 122:1-2, 6a, 8a, 9**

Theme: Greeting the holy city

Outline
Meditation upon returning home from Jerusalem
1   What joy it was to go to the house of the L<small>ORD</small>.
2-5   What awe we felt as we came in sight of the city and stood within its gates, remembering its history and significance.
6   Prayer for the well-being of Jerusalem.

Notes
- Affirmation of Faith
- One of the Song of Ascents (Psalms 120-134).
- Though the title ascribes it to David (not in some ancient manuscripts) it is obviously of a post-exilic origin and use.
- Most Israelites lived in areas where visits to Jerusalem were probably infrequent, three times a year for festivals — Passover, Weeks, Booths. (See Deuteronomy 16:16.) In addition to sacrificial worship, there would be the opportunity to sell one's produce, to buy needs, to listen in a court of law, and for the children something like going to the fair!

For Reflection
- "For the sake of the house of the L<small>ORD</small>, I will seek your good." If we know "the house of the Lord" is not only a place, but a community of worshipers, the whole people of God, the church, the place of God's presence by his Holy Spirit in our day, then what

should be our attitude toward it? What is it to seek good for the church? Do we share the psalmist's spirit?
- Read Luke 19:41-44. Could Jesus have had this psalm in mind when he rode into Jerusalem on Palm Sunday? Why was his "greeting" a sorrowful contrast to the psalmist's? What are "the things that make for peace"?

Prayer

Lord, make us instruments of your peace.
Where there is hatred, let us sow love;
where there is injury, pardon;
where there is discord, union;
where there is doubt, faith;
where there is despair, hope;
where there is darkness, light;
where there is sadness, joy.

Grant that we may not so much seek
to be consoled as to console;
to be understood as to understand;
to be loved as to love.
For it is in giving that we receive;
it is in pardoning that we are pardoned;
and it is in dying that we are born to eternal life.

— **attributed to Saint Francis**

123
To You I Lift Up My Eyes

O you who are enthroned in the heavens!
As the eyes of servants
  look to the hand of their master ...
*So our eyes look to the L*ORD *our God,*
  until he has mercy upon us.
— **Psalm 123:1b-2a, 2c**

Theme: Prayer of the scorned faithful

Outline
1-2 We look to the LORD, like servants to their master, dependent on him for our needs and our directions.
3-4 Have mercy, Lord! We are being treated with contempt!

Notes
- Lament
- One of the Song of Ascents (Psalms 120-134).
- Probably written in Nehemiah's day, when returning exiles expected great things from God but found themselves in humiliating situations, receiving abuse and jeers from the Samaritans and heathen neighbors.
- The "proud" and "at ease" may be those who have no mission in life but to selfishly live it up and look down on the struggling faithful.
- Used on pilgrimage to remind them of God's care in trials and, when scorned, to pray.

For Reflection
- Cruel treatment causes bitterness, resentments, and emotional stress.
- The psalmist looked to God hoping for relief and renewal, his sore need.
- Shall we seek renewal and relief by means of prayer and our worship of the Lord?

Prayer

O God, who hast made man in thine own likeness and who dost love all whom thou hast made: Teach us the unity of thy family and the breadth of thy love. By the example of thy Son, Jesus our Savior, enable us, while loving and serving our own, to enter into the fellowship of the whole human family, and forbid that, from pride of race or hardness of heart, we should despise any for whom Christ died or injure any in whom he lives. Amen.

— from *The Book of Common Prayer*

124
If It Had Not Been The Lord Who Was On Our Side ...

If it had not been the Lord who was on our side,
 when our enemies attacked us,
then they would have swallowed us up alive ...
We have escaped like a bird from the snare ...
Our help is in the name of the Lord,
 who made heaven and earth.
— Psalm 124:2-3a, 7a, 8

Theme: The Savior of Israel

Outline

1-5   Unless God had defended us, we would have gotten swallowed up by enemies.
6-8   Thanks to God for our escape! Renewed confidence for the future.

Notes
- Thanksgiving
- One of the Song of Ascents (Psalms 120-134).
- Read Nehemiah 4:7-23 and 6:15-16 for the background story. As the returned exiles were building the city walls, the heathen jeered, then planned to attack. The psalm is a thanksgiving to God for protecting them.
- The priest introduces the song (v. 1); then the congregation sings it (vv. 2-8).
- Enemies are compared to a monster, a ferocious beast, a sudden flood to sweep them away, or a trapper to ensnare them.

For Reflection
- This is the Christian's experience and thanksgiving, also. God rescues us again and again from many dangers, attacks from the world, the flesh, and the devil.

Prayer
Lord God, we are here today because you have brought us this far, preserved us from many dangers and all the forces of evil that might have destroyed us. We praise you with grateful hearts and with trust and hope. We look forward to the future from your hand of grace. Truly, our redemption comes from him who made heaven and earth, through Jesus Christ our Lord. Amen.

125
Those Who Trust In The LORD Are Like Mount Zion

Those who trust in the LORD are like Mount Zion,
which cannot be moved, but abides forever.
As the mountains surround Jerusalem,
so the LORD surrounds his people ...
— **Psalm 125:1-2a**

Theme: God protects his faithful

Outline
1-3 Our security is God's surrounding presence, our foes will not be allowed to drive us to despair.
4-5 Prayer for the loyal-hearted, and warning of the fate of the disloyal.

Notes
- Affirmation of Faith
- One of the Song of Ascents (Psalms 120-134).
- Read Nehemiah 6 for background.
- "Scepter of wickedness" = the rule of the wicked and heathen powers.
- "Upright in their hearts" = the loyal and sincere.

For Reflection
- The psalmist says (v. 3) that God won't permit the dominion of evil to remain over the land, lest the righteous adopt evil tactics themselves. That would be to counter evil with evil, which is not God's way of overcoming, however popular it is with the world's thinking.
- Jesus warned of the days when "because of the increase of lawlessness, the love of many will grow cold. But the one who endures to the end will be saved." (See Matthew 24:12-13.) Influences and disappointments can make us hard and cynical, withdrawn into self, causing love to grow cold. What can we do to prevent that?

- Saint Paul said, "God is faithful, and he will not let you be tested beyond your strength, but with the testing will also provide the way out so that you may be able to endure it." (See 1 Corinthians 10:13.)
- Bottom line: those who trust in the Lord have God's presence surrounding and protecting them. We may feel utterly trapped, seeing no way out. But we trust God's plan will proceed to its goal, even if we do not see it in this lifetime.

Prayer
Lord God, give to us such faith and good hope in you, that we will not succumb to temptations to evil, nor lose our love in Christ for all people, nor give way to the grave sin of despair. Keep us in fellowship with you for the kingdom you have prepared for us from the foundation of the world, through Jesus Christ our Lord. Amen.

126
When The LORD Restored The Fortress Of Zion

Those who go out weeping,
  bearing the seed for sowing,
shall come home with shouts of joy
  carrying their sheaves.

— Psalm 126:6

Theme: Song of the returning exiles

Outline

1-3   Joy at the incredible marvel of Israel restored to its own land.
4-6   However feeble our efforts seem now, we pray with confidence for the fulfillment of the hope God has given us.

Notes
- Liturgy
- One of the Song of Ascents (Psalms 120-134).
- Read with Psalm 85.
- In 586 BC, Jerusalem fell to the Babylonian Empire, and many Israelites were deported to Babylon. In 539, Cyrus of Persia overcame Babylon practically overnight and in a few years began to allow the exiles to return to their homeland. It was an unforeseen miracle and seemed like a dream to the astonished and overjoyed exiles who began trekking home. Years later, trying to rebuild amid the ruins and finding it difficult, they pray in hope for a prosperity they can only remember.
- "Watercourses of the Negeb" — an arid region south of Judah, with brooks dried up in summer but rushing with water in autumn rains. The psalmist suggests they are only experiencing a trickle yet.
- "Sow in tears" — an ancient near-Eastern custom of weeping when sowing was thought to ensure fertility and a good harvest. Here it is applied to their hope for a more fulfilling restoration.

For Reflection
- When life is difficult, troubles mount, and successes are small if at all, is one to conclude that the gospel has lost its power, or that God has changed toward us? Jesus' greatest work was done with tears and bloody sweat. Saint Paul wrote of his travails to the triumphalist Corinthians, "our bodies had no rest, but we were afflicted in every way — disputes without and fears within. But God, who consoles the downcast, consoled us ..." (2 Corinthians 7:5-6) "... in toil and hardship, through many a sleepless night, hungry and thirsty, often without food, cold and naked, and, besides other things, I am under daily pressure because of my anxiety for all the churches. Who is weak and I am not weak? Who is made to stumble, and I am not indignant?" (2 Corinthians 11:27-29).
- Charles Spurgeon wrote: "Weeping times are suitable for sowing ... Instead of stopping our sowing because of our weeping, let us redouble our efforts because the season is propitious."[1]

Prayer
> *"Come and help us, Lord Jesus. A vision of your face will brighten us, but to feel your Spirit touching us will make us vigorous. Oh! for the leaping and walking of the man born lame. May we today dance with holy joy, like David before the ark of God. May a holy exhilaration take possession of every part of us; may we be glad in the Lord; may our mouth be filled with laughter, and our tongue with singing, 'for the Lord hath done great things for us whereof we are glad.'"*[2]

---

1. Charles Spurgeon, *Faith's Checkbook* (Chicago: Moody Publishers, 1987), p. 184.

2. Charles Spurgeon, quoted in Horton Davies, *The Communion of Saints* (Grand Rapids, Michigan: Eerdmans, 1990), p. 79.

127
Unless The Lord Builds The House

It is in vain that you rise up early
  and go late to rest,
eating the bread of anxious toil;
  for he gives sleep to his beloved.

— **Psalm 127:2**

Theme: A family needs God's blessing

Outline
1-2   Without God, anxious toil is futile. God gives peace and rest to those who count on his love.
3-4   A family is one of God's rich blessings.

Notes
- Wisdom
- One of the Song of Ascents (Psalms 120-134).
- The title says "Of Solomon," perhaps meaning "in the style and spirit of Solomon," with similarities to the book of Proverbs. It reflects the circumstances of Nehemiah's time, where there was much house-building. The first chapter of Haggai provides an interesting background for the message of the psalm.
- "Enemies in the gate" — the city gate was where the Justice of the Peace held court, and citizens met for business and legal issues. There an enemy might parley before engaging in battle.
- Families in which greed, selfishness, fear, and jealousy are unchecked by covenant loyalty will fail. Those with the Lord can experience peace and rest, his gift.

For Reflection
- Charles Spurgeon writes: "Ours is not a life of anxious care, but of happy faith. Our heavenly Father will supply the wants of His own children, and He knoweth what we have need of before we ask Him. We may therefore go to our beds at the proper hour, and not wear ourselves out by sitting up late to plot, and plan, and contrive. If we have learned to rely upon our God we shall

not lie awake with fear gnawing at our hearts; but we shall leave our care with the Lord, our meditation of Him shall be sweet, and He will give us refreshing sleep."[1]

Prayer
Lord God, you have given us good reason to rest in you. You gave us Jesus, through whom we have peace with you. We rejoice in our hope of sharing your glory. Give us faith to realize that, having dealt with our greatest need with such extravagant love, you can deal with our lesser ones, too, in ways that keep us with you unto eternal life, through Jesus Christ our Lord. Amen.

---

1. Charles Spurgeon, *Faith's Checkbook* (Chicago: Moody Publishers, 1987), p. 184.

128
Happy Is Everyone Who Fears The Lord

Happy is everyone who fears the Lord,
  who walks in his ways ...
  ... it shall go well with you.
— **Psalm 128:1, 2b**

Theme: A marriage needs God's blessing

Outline

1-3 The happy family is a result and reward of godliness.
4-6 Blessings on the ones who revere the Lord.

Notes
- Wisdom
- One of the Song of Ascents (Psalms 120-134).
- This is a companion to Psalm 127. An encouragement to godliness for pilgrim parents and their youth going to Jerusalem and to Christian pilgrims going to the New Jerusalem.
- "Vine" = fruitful, beautiful, precious, dependent, needing care.
- "Olive shoots" = fresh and full of promise.
- "Around your table" = a picture of good fellowship in the family.
- The priest would give the blessing (vv. 5-6), which came from Zion (God's earthly dwelling), promising prosperity for Jerusalem (not in mere material sense, but spiritual, as the people seek to fulfill their mission from the Lord to the world). "Your children's children" could mean not only the grandchildren but also a long line of godly progeny to come.

For Reflection
- Our Lutheran baptism service is as beautiful and awe-inspiring as any such service to be found anywhere. Just to think seriously and earnestly of the words and meaningful rubrics prompts one to pray for the baptized and, in the case of infants, the parents, God's foremost representatives to the child. They need the prayers, encouragement, and blessings of the whole church.

Prayer
Lord God, give to parents the faith, the love, and the courage they need to provide an example to their children of faithfulness to you and to one another. May their homes be marked with reverence, freedom, and good fellowship with you and with one another through the love of Jesus Christ, your Son our Lord. Amen.

129
Often Have They Attacked Me From My Youth

"Often have they attacked me from my youth ...
yet they have not prevailed against me ..."
May all who hate Zion
be put to shame and turned backward.
— Psalm 129:1a, 2b, 5

Theme: God keeps Israel from destruction

Outline

1-4 Through Israel's many ups and downs, the LORD has not let it perish.
5-7 Confident hope and prayer that the enemies of Zion shall be turned back before their wicked schemes mature.

Notes
- Affirmation of Faith
- One of the Song of Ascents (Psalms 120-134).
- "Plowed on my back" — a metaphor of cruel treatment, picturing the slave's back lacerated by the lash.
- "Cords" — things that fasten the yoke on the oxen's necks, symbol of servitude.
- "The blessing of the LORD be upon you!" is the kind greeting of passersby to reapers at their work, and the response received, "We bless you in the name of the LORD!" (See Ruth 2:4 for an example.)

For Reflection
- Think of the sufferings of the Jews, not only those of ancient time, but also of modern times. The call of God to be his people has been, and always is a call to share God's suffering heart for the world.
- We can suffer with him and for him, as he did and does for us, or we can suffer from our own choices of sinful pride and willfulness.

Prayer

Pope John XXIII (1881-1963) gave Christians a good example in making this prayer (and publicizing it) for the whole church:

O God, we are conscious that many centuries of blindness have blinded our eyes so that we no longer see the beauty of thy chosen people, nor recognize in their faces the features of our privileged brethren. We realize that the mark of Cain stands upon our foreheads. Across the centuries our brother Abel has lain in the blood which we drew or which we caused to be shed by forgetting thy love. Forgive us for the curse we falsely attached to their name as Jews. Forgive us for crucifying thee a second time in their flesh. For we knew not what we did. Amen.
— **quoted in** *The Oxford Book of Prayer*, **#366, ed. G. Appleton, 1985**

130
Out Of The Depths, I Cry To You, O LORD

I wait for the Lord, my soul waits,
and in his word I hope ...
O Israel, hope in the LORD!
For with the LORD there is steadfast love,
and with him is great power to redeem.
— Psalm 130:5, 7

Theme: Waiting for redemption (*De Profundis*)

Outline
1-4   Overwhelmed with guilt and suffering, he pleads with God to hear and to forgive him.
5-8   Knowing God's revealed character, he is willing to wait in anticipation (hope) for a great redemption that is surely coming.

Notes
- Penitential
- One of the Song of Ascents (Psalms 120-134).
- While this could be a nation's prayer (Nehemiah 1:4-11), it is especially meant for an individual. Brief, eloquent, powerful, a perfect prayer for a penitent sinner.
- One of four psalms Luther called "Pauline Psalms" (32; 51; 130; 143) and also one of the seven Penitential Psalms.
- Saint Augustine had verse 4 written on the wall of his room as he lay dying.
- "Depths" = one's own private hell as well as fear of God's judgment.
- "Revered" — forgiveness restores the fellowship that was broken.
- "There is no picture here of the proud humanity that the Greeks valued so much; rather it is the true humanity of humility."[1]

For Reflection
- From Luther: "Now there are some who want to set the goal, appoint the hour and measure, and prescribe to God how they are to be helped. And if they do not experience this, they despair; or, if possible, they seek help elsewhere. These do not

tarry and wait for the Lord. God is supposed to wait for them, be ready at once, and help exactly as they themselves have designed. Those who wait for the Lord, however, ask for mercy; but they leave it to God's gracious will when, how, where, and by what means He helps them."[2]

Prayer
Lord God, with grateful hearts we praise you for the Savior who shared our horrible times of testing and the temptations to despair, who knows the depths of our private hells, and who will bring us out of them into the pure, clean, holy, and bright glory of your kingdom. We will wait with keen anticipation for the great redemption that is coming from you, through Jesus Christ our Lord. Amen.

---

1. George A. F. Knight, *Psalms*, Vol. 2 (New York: Cambridge Publishing, 1957), p. 290.

2. Martin Luther, *Luther's Works*, Vol. 14 (St. Louis: Concordia Publishing House, 1956), p. 192.

131
O Lord, My Heart Is Not Lifted Up

O Lord, my heart is not lifted up ...
I do not occupy myself with things
  too great and too marvelous for me.
But I have calmed and quieted my soul.
— **Psalm 131:1a, 1c-2a**

Theme: The calmed and quieted soul

Outline
1. I have renounced haughtiness and ambitious schemes (with their attendant storms of passion) and chosen patient, quiet trust in the Lord.
2. I have found peace and security, like a humble child in its mother's arms, weaned and contented.
3. Let Israel so hope in the Lord.

Notes
- Affirmation of Faith
- One of the Song of Ascents (Psalms 120-134).
- In the return and restoration period, the great triumphs for Israel promised by the prophets had been interpreted in a high and grandiose way. Now they have a humility born out of penitence.
- A follow-up of Psalm 130. They had to unload ambitions, dreams, and in their lowly position accept small blessings. To their surprise the ensuing peace was truly marvelous.

For Reflection
- The psalmist found a formula for serenity and for relief from possibly neurotic ambition. If we translate his statements into today's tensions, which we feel about ourselves, our lives, and about God, we may see our way to relief and serenity.
  a. Accept our limitations (like Paul suggested in Philippians 2:3-4).
  b. Dethrone pride and humble ourselves (Philippians 2:5-11).
  c. Put our hope (goal) in the Lord (Philippians 4:4-7).

Prayer
Lord Jesus, you call to us weary and heavy-laden people to come to you and learn of you, who are gentle and humble of heart. Like a calmed and quieted child in a loving mother's arms, may we find renewing rest in you, bearing your mild yoke. Amen.

132
O Lord, Remember In David's Favor

For the Lord has chosen Zion;
  he has desired it for his habitation:
"This is my resting place forever ...
There ... I have prepared a lamp
  for my anointed one."
— **Psalm 132:13-14a, 17**

Theme: David and Zion — elected of God

Outline
1-10   Prayer of the people concerning David
       1-5   Remember David's hardships and his oath to provide a dwelling place for the Lord.
       6-7   How the people helped and brought the Ark to Zion.
       8-10   Plea for God to take possession of his house, that its priests be righteous and the people jubilant.
11-18   God's response in two oracles
       11-12   Summary of God's promises to David. (See 2 Samuel 7:2-17.)
       13-18   God has chosen Zion as his dwelling place, with blessings to come. (See 1 Kings 11:36; 15:4; 2 Samuel 21:17.)

Notes
- Royal Messianic
- One of the Song of Ascents (Psalms 120-134).
- Back from exile, the temple rebuilt, but now what about God's promises? What about the house of David? A king from his line? The psalm was a reminder that God had not forgotten his promises, his "anointed one."
- Truly a messianic psalm, looking forward to the fulfillment of God's promises to David. "Such an expression of Messianic hope was most natural for the pilgrims going up to Jerusalem for the feast and recalling all the memories connected with the 'city of David.'"

- Ark of the Covenant (2 Samuel 6) = symbol of God's presence.
- "Ephrathah" was probably the name of the area where the Ark was kept (v. 6). (See 1 Samuel 7:1-2.)
- "Horn" = symbol of strength and also of the king.
- "Lamp" is a metaphor for preservation of the dynasty of David (v. 17).

For Reflection
- Zion meant God's dwelling place. After building the temple on the hill called Zion, then transferring the Ark to it, the name came to stand for the temple. There God could be approached in a special way.
- This is an example of the particularism of biblical revelation. While God can be approached throughout his creation, and heaven itself cannot contain him (1 Kings 8:27), yet God chooses to be at a particular place of his electing. Just as in Christ, "... the Word became flesh and lived among us, and we have seen his glory, the glory as of a father's only son, full of grace and truth" (John 1:14).

Prayer
Lord God, we praise you for your redeeming purpose. You gave us from David's line the Savior of the world. You make your dwelling in the new Zion, the people of the Lord. May your anointed one, Jesus Christ, dwell in our hearts by faith, clothe us in righteousness, satisfy the poor, and to serve you at our various stations with faithfulness and joy. Amen.

133
How Very Good And Pleasant It Is ...

How very good and pleasant it is
  when kindred live together in unity! ...
It is like the dew of Hermon,
  which falls on the mountains of Zion.
For there the Lord ordained his blessing,
  life forevermore.

— Psalm 133:1, 3

Theme: God's blessing on the loving family

Outline

1	How good and pleasant is family unity.
2	First simile: it is costly, like the "precious oil" anointing the priest, symbol of joy, celebration. (See Psalm 45:7.)
3a	Second simile: it is like dew on the mountains, gentle, refreshing, renewing life.
3b	Zion — where God commands his blessing: life forevermore!

Note
- Liturgy
- One of the Song of Ascents (Psalms 120-134).

For Reflection
- Kindred can mean one's family and relatives, as well as one's fellow believers in covenant with God.
- Each happy home, and each loving congregation is a far-reaching blessing to the whole community.
- Where can unity (concord, mutual love) be found? (See John 17:21; Ephesians 4:1-6; Philippians 2:2.)
- How valuable is this unity? (See John 13:34-35.)
- How costly is it? (See Ephesians 2:14-16; Colossians 1:19-20; Galatians 5:24-26.)

Prayer
O God, who art our dwelling-place in all generations: Look with favor upon the homes of our land; enfold husbands and wives, parents and children, in the bonds of thy pure love; and so bless our homes, that they may be a shelter for the defenceless, a bulwark for the tempted, a resting-place for the weary, and a foretaste of our eternal home in thee; through Jesus Christ our Lord. Amen.
— from *Service Book and Hymnal*, 1958, p. 273

134
Come, Bless The LORD, All You Servants Of The LORD

Come, bless the LORD, all you servants of the LORD,
who stand by night in the house of the LORD! ...
May the LORD ...
bless you from Zion.

— **Psalm 134:1, 3**

Theme: A closing evening liturgy

Outline
Closing liturgical dialogue of pilgrims and temple ministers
1-2   Hymn by congregation, a call to ministering priests to "Bless the Lord."
3   Response by the priest, a benediction: "The LORD bless you from Zion!"

Notes
- Liturgy
- One of the Song of Ascents (Psalms 120-134).
- This liturgical blessing brings to an end the series of "Songs of Ascents" (Psalms 120-134).
- "Who stand by night" = assigned for priestly service at night.
- "Lifted hands" = a common gesture of prayer.

For Reflection
- Note the reciprocal action: worshipers praying in support of their ministers, and ministers praying for their people. How often should one pray for the pastor? Should pastors over a space of time have a prayer for each individual member of his congregation? What might that do for the pastor? The people?
- "The Lord bless you from Zion" means "from the church, the Christ community bringing the gospel to you and your family, and your community." Why is your church absolutely and uniquely important for you and your loved ones?

Prayer

Lord God, bless our pastors and our congregation. They are each needed by you, and we need them. They are important for your redeeming purpose and therefore important for us.

Bless pastors and teachers in the church with the renewing gift of your Holy Spirit. Speak to their hearts so that you may speak to ours through them. Bless each member of our congregation, each loved and sought by you that with one heart and voice even we may bless you, through Jesus Christ our Lord.

Blessed be God! Blessed be Father, Son, and Holy Spirit! Amen.

135
Praise The LORD!
Praise The Name Of The LORD

Praise the LORD!
Praise the name of the LORD;
give praise, O servants of the LORD ...
For I know that the LORD is great;
our Lord is above all gods.
Whatever the LORD pleases he does,
in heaven and on earth,
in the seas and all deeps ...
For the LORD will vindicate his people;
and have compassion on his servants.
— Psalm 135:1, 5-6, 14

Theme: The surpassing greatness of Yahweh

Outline

1-4   Call to praise the LORD, who elected Jacob (Israel) for himself.
5-7   His greatness is seen in his power over nature.
8-14 His greatness is to be seen in Israel's actual experience of redemption.
15-18 By contrast, the heathen gods are mute and powerless.
19-21 Blessed be the LORD from Zion!

Notes
- Praise — Creation/History
- The psalm is a mosaic of fragments from other psalms, the law, and the prophets.
- "Your name, O Lord" = God's reputation, conveyed through the recital and memory of his deeds; his revelation.
- "Vindicate" = justify, exonerate, show to be right.

For Reflection
- What is it to praise God? Does God want compliments? No. He wants us to enjoy him, exult in his grace and love and

power, and to have a part in his activity with gratitude, gladness, and anticipation. But modern man has been robbed of this revelation.
- Science has no consideration of God in its descriptions. Historians take for granted that they need not consider God in their telling of the past. Psychologists avoid consideration of God in their efforts to understand and interpret the human psyche. Against all this skepticism and all the rivals to our faith in the ideologies of the day and the idol of greed, the psalmist calls us to delight in God because of his power shown in the created universe, and the historical events that called Israel into being.
- The Christian knows the greatest reason for the praise of God: the gift of Jesus Christ to the world. His life, death, resurrection, and giving of the Holy Spirit are the most awesome and revelatory events in all history. Do these "mighty acts of God" call forth grateful joy, confident hope, and reverent yielding to him, our Lord?

Prayer
Lord God, you have given us good reason to trust you and to yield to you our hearts and lives. But both heart and mind are in bondage, and our knowledge of you is lifeless until your Spirit makes it live. As we read and ponder your word, may your Holy Spirit open our eyes to see your glory, our hearts to exult in you, and our lives to show it in humble service for you, through Jesus Christ our Lord. Amen.

136
O Give Thanks To The Lord, For He Is Good

O give thanks to the Lord, for he is good,
  for his steadfast love endures forever ...
who alone does great wonders,
  for his steadfast love endures forever ...
It is he who remembered us in our low estate,
  for his steadfast love endures forever.
— Psalm 136:1, 4, 23

Theme: A liturgical thanksgiving

Outline
1-3 Give thanks to the Lord, the God of gods and Lord of lords:
4-9 creator of all things,
10-22 deliverer of Israel, giver of the promised land,
23-25 redeemer of his people from exile, provider of food for all the living, and
26 the God of heaven.

Notes
- Praise — Creation/History
- The Great Hallel.
- A liturgical thanksgiving, each verse's refrain was sung as a response to the singer (choir or priest). (See Ezra 3:11; 2 Chronicles 7:3, 6 for examples.)
- "Steadfast love" = (*chesed*) the word that tells the nature of God's covenant love. This word is used 26 times in this psalm, 114 times in the whole psalter. It is intended to impress upon the people God's loyal faithfulness to them, an unmerited kindness, and to call forth their loyal faithfulness to him.
- This is another example of the "Theology of Recital" in which worshipers cited the saving acts of God, such as we do in the Apostles' and Nicene Creeds.

For Reflection
- After saying, "for his steadfast love endures forever" 26 times, the phrase is not forgotten. Instead of merely mouthing words, the repetition (memorizing), can cause us to think about its significance for us. Then the Spirit can give an "Aha! Now I see!" experience.
- Memorizing one's favorite psalm or scripture passage can become a means of meditating on the word of God, and the passage becomes an inward treasure instantly available for help in temptations to fear, doubt, despair, and other common assaults on our faith and hope.

Prayer
Lord God, you alone do great wonders. You are faithful to us. Your great wonders are to be seen in the glories of creation, the story of Israel, and your provident care for all life. Most of all your great love is shown in your overcoming our death, bearing away our sin, calling us to life with you through Jesus Christ. We unite with Israel of old, the church through the ages, and the hosts of heaven in giving you thanks and praise, for your steadfast love endures forever, through Jesus Christ our Lord. Amen.

137
By The Rivers Of Babylon

By the rivers of Babylon
    there we sat down and there we wept
    when we remembered Zion.
For there our captors
    asked us for songs,
and our tormentors asked for mirth, saying,
    "Sing us one of the songs of Zion!"
— Psalm 137:1, 3

Theme: Song of the exiles

Outline
1-3   In exile we were weeping instead of singing.
4-6   How could we sing — and forget Jerusalem?
7-9   Lord, bring vengeance upon Edom and Babylon.

Notes
- Lament
- Written before or soon after the close of the exile.
- Rivers = Babylon's many willow-lined canals and streams.
- Mirth = entertainment, not spiritual witness sought by their working gang leaders.
- Edom, neighbor to the east, descended from Esau, with age-long hostilities.
- The barbarous custom of Oriental warfare spared neither women nor children — much like modern warfare (v. 9).
- An example of the "songs of Zion" is Psalm 46. Read it and see one reason why they could not sing it!
- A railroad runs through the desert today from Baghdad, passes a small watering station with an arrow pointing into the desert, "to Babylon." It is now a mound or *tel* in the desert.

For Reflection
- With the temple and city of Jerusalem in ruins, they must have asked, "Where was God? What about his promises? Are we no better off than the heathen with their helpless gods?" Yet they prayed and kept the faith! This is amazing.

- When our world falls apart, do we have faith to still trust the Lord? (See 1 Corinthians 15:19.)
- Instead of wanting vengeance, pray for the enemies, as Jesus said. Pray for God to restrain and convert them!

Prayer
Lord God, you have transferred us into the kingdom of your Son and made us citizens of heaven. We are now far from home, living truly in a familiar but very "strange" land. But we will sing your praises here in anticipation of the glorious day that is coming, and in hope that your Spirit will use us to bring others to praise you, too, through Jesus Christ our Lord. Amen.

138
I Give You Thanks, O Lord

I give you thanks, O Lord, with my whole heart;
  before the gods I sing your praise ...
  for you have exalted your name and your word
  above everything ...
The Lord will fulfill his purpose for me;
  your steadfast love, O Lord, endures forever.
  Do not forsake the work of your hands.
  — **Psalm 138:1, 2c, 8**

Theme: Seven reasons for wholehearted thanks to God

Outline
1-3   Amidst the idolatrous pomp of the world, I thank you, Lord, for your covenant love and faithfulness to me.
4-6   I look forward to the day when heathen nations will have learned to sing of your ways.
7-8   Amidst troubles, I look forward to the fulfillment of your redeeming purpose for me.

Notes
- Thanksgiving
- God's name (his character, his reputation) and God's word (his revelation to man) are exalted above everything, the supreme blessings for the world (v. 2).
- This is a missionary psalm, looking forward to the salvation of the world (v. 4).
- "The work of your hands" = the nation of Israel, the individual who wrote the psalm and the one praying it, and all creation (v. 8).

For Reflection
- What are the seven great reasons for heartfelt gratitude to God? Verse 8 is a great promise and prayer for everyone to use. "God will keep me going until he has fulfilled his purpose for me." And when death comes, he will keep on working in me and through me!

- Every person in the covenant of salvation is the handwork of God. "We are what he has made us, created in Christ Jesus for good works, which God prepared beforehand to be our way of life" (Ephesians 2:10). "He who began a good work among you will bring it to completion by the day of Jesus Christ" (Philippians 1:6).

Prayer
Lord God, in the midst of heathenism and of troubles, we thank you that you have begun a good work in us. With the psalmist we are confident as we anticipate the fulfillment of your purpose for us, for both the lowliest of humankind as well as for kings yet afar off needing to hear your word. You will not forsake the work of your pierced hands, O Christ. Amen.

139
O Lord, You Have Searched Me And Known Me

You discern my thoughts from far away ...
and are acquainted with all my ways.
If I ascend to heaven, you are there;
if I make my bed in Sheol, you are there ...
Search me, O God, and know my heart ...
See if there is any wicked way in me,
and lead me in the way everlasting.
— Psalm 139:2b, 3b, 8, 23a, 24

Theme: God: all-knowing, ever-present, powerful!

Outline

1-6	You know, Lord, my every thought and action!
7-12	You are there — present wherever I go!
13-18	You created me — planned for me before I was born!
19-22	Why do you tolerate evil? I want to hate it like you hate it.
23-24	Keep on searching and testing my heart and my ways, root out all wickedness and lead me your way.

Notes
- Wisdom
- One of the greatest of the psalms. "This is one of the most profound statements of personal religion in the Psalter."[1]
- God's power extends over Sheol, the abode of the dead! Why not also the hells we can make in our lives here? God can bring us out of their darkness into his light (v. 8).
- "The depths of the earth" = the womb, dark, and mysterious (v. 15).
- "As yet there were none of them" — no pre-existence (v. 16).
- "Precious" = incomprehensible, overwhelming (v. 17).

For Reflection
- How are the evildoers described? (vv. 18-21). These throw a monkey wrench into God's marvelous works of creation, bringing sorrow and ruin. He wants God to get rid of them. Should not a Christian feel a burning indignation against evil?

- Pondering this, the psalmist recognizes, as we must too, his own complicity in it all. God has prepared a way to be rid of his enemies in a way yet unknown to the psalmist: to reconcile them in Christ and make them into friends who love him. This is the way God will lead his people in answer to the prayer of verses 23-24: searching the heart in all its sinfulness, convicting of sin with tests and trials, bringing the sinner to faith in the one crucified for us all, and to reconciliation through his cross.

Prayer

Lord God, you know all about us; even our subconscious is open to you. You descend into the hells of our sinful making, and you can lead us out of them. Which is more difficult for you — to create us or to re-create us in Christ? Our grateful praise goes to you for your entering into our woe, sharing it with us, and bringing us forgiveness and life through our Lord Jesus Christ. Amen.

---

1. Arnold Rhodes, *Psalms — The Layman's Study Bible*, Vol. 9 (Louisville: Westminster John Knox Press, 1962), p. 181.

140
Deliver Me, O Lord, From Evildoers

Deliver me, O Lord, from evildoers;
  protect me from those who are violent ...
O Lord, my Lord, my strong deliverer,
  you have covered my head in the day of battle ...
I know that the Lord maintains the cause of the needy
  and executes justice for the poor.
— **Psalm 140:1, 7, 12**

Theme: Prayer for protection

Outline

1-8   Prayer for deliverance from evildoers.
9-11 Prayer for their evils to overtake them.
12-13 God will maintain his cause for the poor and the righteous.

Notes
- Lament
- Psalms 140-143 are a group with similar characteristics:
  a. All bear the name of David.
  b. All are similar in thought and language.
  c. All reflect the same circumstances — one subject to the attacks and plotting of wicked men.
  d. Davidic authorship is questioned by scholars.

For Reflection
- In verses 1-5, how does the psalmist describe the character, the methods, and the purpose of the evildoers?
- What does the psalmist pray for?
- What sustains his faith? (vv. 6-8, 12-13).
- The New Testament believers' experience of conflict with evil is dealt with in many passages. (See Ephesians 6:10-13; Romans 12:9-21.)

Prayer
Lord God, protect us from the temptations of the devil, and from the injustices and cruelties of the wicked. Maintain your cause and uphold justice and truth in our lives, through Jesus Christ our Lord. Amen.

141
I Call Upon You, O LORD, Come Quickly

Let my prayer be counted as incense before you,
and the lifting up of my hands as an evening sacrifice ...
But my eyes are turned toward you, O GOD, my Lord;
in you I seek refuge; do not leave me defenseless.
— **Psalm 141:2, 8**

Theme: Prayer for protection from the lure of sin

Outline

1-2   Hear my prayer; let it be counted as the evening sacrifice.
3-5   Help me resist temptations to sin.
6-7   The wicked will find out how wrong they were (meaning uncertain).
8-10 Prayer for God to keep him from being trapped by them, and to let the ways of the wicked be self-defeating.

Notes
- Lament
- From early times this psalm has been used in the vespers or evening service in the church.
- The psalmist (a Levite?) knows, even if he can't be in Jerusalem for the daily sacrifice, he can approach God as truly in prayer as if assisting in the temple.
- Verses 6-7 are hard to translate, and various meanings have been given to fit them with the context.
- "Their delicacies" = offers.
- "Oil of the wicked" = smooth talk.
- Being thrown over a cliff was a common form of execution in the ancient world (v. 7).

For Reflection
- The psalmist prays for correction in order to be kept from sin's hold. By nature we don't like correction. It's a feature of our sinful nature to dread humiliation and to seek to establish our

own righteousness instead of accepting righteousness as a credited gift of God, to be enjoyed with humility (honesty) and gratitude.
- See Proverbs 9:8; 15:32; Hebrews 12:5; Revelation 3:19.

Prayer
Protect us, O God, from the lure of sin and the ways of the sinful. Enable us by your Holy Spirit to refuse the proffered delicacies and smooth talk of the wicked, and to turn our attention to you and to your blessed will for us in Christ Jesus our Lord. Amen.

142
With My Voice I Cry To The Lord

I pour out my complaint before him;
I tell my trouble before him.
When my spirit is faint,
you know my way ...
no one cares for me ...
Give heed to my cry,
for I am brought very low.

— Psalm 142:2-3a, 4c, 6a

Theme: A great example of prayer for the discouraged or the depressed

Outline
1-2 I am laying out my distress before the Lord.
3-4 Lord, you know my situation and my helplessness.
5-7 Bring me out of this "prison" so I can thank you and the righteous can share with me.

Notes
- Lament
- A "Maskil of David" — a religious instruction for meditation and prayer based on David's experience in the cave of Adullum in 1 Samuel 22 or the cave of Engedi in 1 Samuel 24.
- Note his desperate situation (vv. 3, 4, 6, 7a).
- This psalm was on the lips of Saint Francis when he died on October 3, 1226.
- See a Christian application of this in 2 Corinthians 1:8-11.

For Reflection
- This psalm deals with the experience Luther called *Anfechtung* (for which there is no English equivalent), a time when one's faith is being attacked such that sin, fear, guilt, or troubled conscience tempt one to despair.
- Luther says in such circumstances one must:
    a. not rely on self or one's feelings but on the words offered in God's name;
    b. not imagine he's the only one suffering like this;

   c. be ready to yield to God's will;
   d. pray, "I will pour out my complaint before him";
   e. realize blessings lie under such a trial, itself a sign of God's love; and
   f. never doubt the promise of our faithful God.
Remember our sins are all paid by Christ![1]

Prayer

> *O Lord, take from me that sorrow which the love of self may produce from my sufferings, and from my unsuccessful hopes and designs in this world, while regardless of Thy glory; but create in me a sorrow resembling Thine. Let me not henceforth desire health or life, except to spend them for Thee, with Thee, and in Thee....*
>   **— from Blaise Pascal, d. 1662**

---

1. Martin Luther, *Luther's Works — Devotional Writings I*, Vol. 42, ed. Martin O. Dietrich and Helmut T. Lehman (Philadelphia: Fortress Press, 1969), pp. 183-186.

143
Hear My Prayer, O LORD

Do not enter into judgment with your servant,
  for no one living is righteous before you ...
  my heart within me is appalled ...
  my soul thirsts for you like a parched land ...
Teach me to do your will,
  for you are my God.
Let your good spirit lead me
  on a level path.
— **Psalm 143:2, 4b, 6b, 10**

Theme: A cry for grace

Outline
1-2   Acknowledging his unrighteousness, he pleads for mercy.
3-4   His horrible situation causes him alarm.
5-6   Thinking of God's doings for Israel in the past makes him long the more for God to show his redeeming power.
7-12 He prays for God to deliver him, to teach and lead him, and to put an end to his enemies.

Notes
- Penitential
- One of the seven Penitential Psalms (6; 32; 38; 51; 102; 130; 143).
- Attributed to David, but verses 7-12 are a collection of memorable statements from earlier psalms.
- Note the basis of his appeal for God to grant his requests (vv. 1, 7, 12).
- Note his specific requests (vv. 1, 2, 7-12).
- Saint Paul uses this psalm in his exposition of God's righteousness (Romans 1-3).

For Reflection
- From Luther: "Every psalm, all Scripture, calls to grace, extols grace, searches for Christ, and praises only God's work, while rejecting all the works of man. Therefore this psalm ... speaks the same language."

"Here it should be noted that the little words 'Thy faith' and 'Thy righteousness' do not refer to the faith and righteousness with which God believes and is righteous, as some have thought, but to the grace whereby God works faith in us and makes us righteous."

"The proud in heart will not stand for it that their work and righteousness is regarded as nothing ... Spiritual pride is the last and deepest vice."[1]

Prayer
Lord God, no one living is righteous before you. But to those in darkness you bring the light of your salvation and make known your love. Teach us the way we should think and live in such grace, your Holy Spirit leading us to do your will, through him who is our wisdom and righteousness, our sanctification and redemption, Jesus Christ our Lord. Amen.

---

1. Martin Luther, *Luther's Works*, Vol. 14 (St. Louis: Concordia Publishing House, 1956), pp. 196, 197, 205.

144
Blessed Be The LORD, My Rock

Blessed be the LORD ...
my rock and my fortress,
my stronghold and my deliverer ...
O LORD, what are human beings that you regard them,
or mortals that you think of them?
— Psalm 144:1a, 2a, 3

Theme: Save the king — bless the people

Outline
1-2   Praise the Lord — giver of victory.
3-4   How marvelous that God should think of man who is weak and shortlived.
5-8   Prayer for victory over enemies.
9-11 Thanksgiving in anticipation of the needed victory.
12-15 Prayer for Israel's prosperity and protection.

Notes
- Royal Messianic — Wisdom
- "Of David" = like David's psalms, with quotes from them and other scriptures.
- "His servant David" has become a messianic title (v. 10).
- Note the abrupt transition to this descriptive blessing, a passage unlike any previous psalm (vv. 12-15).

For Reflection
- As in Psalm 8 and elsewhere, the humility or condescension of God to be caring and concerned for man and for individuals is astounding to contemplate. The revelation of this truth in Israel's history gives boldness in praying, asking great things of God.
- Saint Paul notes this in Ephesians 1:3-14.

Prayer
Lord God, you bow your heavens and come down to us. You teach us to fight the good fight of faith and give us victory against the forces of evil, all that would destroy us. Give your church confidence in the weapons you provide — your Word and your Spirit, that we may show your ways to the blessing of the world, through him who won for all the great victory, our Lord Jesus Christ. Amen.

145
I Will Extole You, My God And King

Every day I will bless you,
*   and praise your name forever and ever ...*
All your works shall give thanks to you, O LORD ...
They shall speak of the glory of your kingdom,
*   and tell of your power,*
to make known to all people your mighty deeds ...
The eyes of all look to you,
*   and you give them their food in due season.*
*   — Psalm 145:2, 10a, 11-12a, 15*

Theme: "For the kingdom, the power, and the glory are yours, now and forever" — a glorious doxology

Notes
- Praise — Acrostic
- An Acrostic psalm (each two lines begin with a different letter of the Hebrew alphabet), where the language, grammar, and dependence on other scripture passages show it to be not by David but post-exilic in origin.
- From here to the end of the psalter, all the psalms are songs of praise.
- This psalm celebrates the universality and eternity of God's kingdom.
- Used liturgically in the synagogue, where it was recited morning and evening. In the ancient church it was used at midday meals. Verses 15-16 have been a table grace used for centuries.
- The Daily Lectionary recommends this is to be used with the Psalm of the Day each Monday.

For Reflection
- There are fifteen to twenty different reasons for praising the Lord in the 21 verses. What are they?
- Who praises God? Find five categories of praises.
- How does one praise God? Find seven ways mentioned. How shall we do it?

Prayer
Lord God, open our heart and our lips that our mouths shall tell and sing of your wondrous love to all the world. Take away our unholy diffidence and give us that boldness with humbleness of heart to give an account to others of the hope and joy you give to us, day after day, through the gospel of Jesus Christ, your Son, our Savior and Lord. Amen.

146
Praise The LORD!
Praise The LORD, O My Soul

I will praise the LORD as long as I live;
I will sing praises to my God all my life long.
Do not put your trust in ... mortals ...
Happy are those whose help is the God of Jacob,
whose hope is in the LORD their God ...
The LORD lifts up those who are bowed down ...
The LORD will reign forever.
— Psalm 146:2-3a, 5, 8b, 10a

Theme: Praise the true helper — the Lord

Outline

1-2   Pledge to praise God throughout life.
3-4   Warning not to trust mortals (prince today and dust tomorrow).
5-6   Happy are those whose help and hope in life is the Lord.
7-9   He is the one who saves the needy.

Notes
- Praise — Creation/History
- One of the Hallelujah Psalms (146-150).
- This is the first of the five Hallelujah Psalms (Psalms 146-150). They begin and end with the Hebrew "Hallelujah" ("praise Yahweh"). They are also called the *Laudate* Psalms (from Latin).
- Liturgical — this was used each morning in the synagogue.
- The Daily Lectionary suggests this is to be used with the Psalm of the Day each Tuesday.

For Reflection
- We can't help seeing the emphasis on the Lord's social concern. List those mentioned of society for whom God is concerned. Then read Matthew 11:2-5 for Jesus' own appraisal of his messianic credentials and his concern.
- "Prison" can stand for various kinds of suffering, for the weak, and for those who do not yet know the gospel. "Blind" can include the spiritually ignorant, the helpless, or the insensitive.

"Orphans" can be the unloved of all ages, the lonely or the most vulnerable.
- Notice the wicked are brought to ruin — another example of the character of the Lord. (What if God didn't care?)
- "We must ever keep in mind the two thoughts — God the Creator of the universe, which came into being at His word; God the Redeemer staggering beneath a load that crushes Him as He goes from Jerusalem to Calvary; so far harder is it to redeem men from selfishness to love than to create the wheeling systems of the stars."[1]

Prayer
Lord God, your concern for people whom we are quick to ignore shames us. Forgive us for our small hearts, and make them into great hearts, with a larger capacity for compassion, your kind of love, that our praises might resound more faithfully with all the company of heaven, through Jesus Christ our Lord. Amen.

---

1. William Temple, *Readings In St. John's Gospel* (London: MacMillan, 1950), p. 365.

147
Praise The LORD!
How Good It Is To Sing Praises To Our God

Praise the LORD!
How good it is to sing praises to our God ...
He heals the brokenhearted
and binds up their wounds ...
but the LORD takes pleasure in those who fear him,
in those who hope in his steadfast love.
— **Psalm 147:1a, 3, 11**

Theme: The Lord cares for his creation

Outline
1-2   Praise the LORD who restores Jerusalem.
3-6   He lifts up those cast down — the mighty Lord!
7-11 Sing his praises. He who loves us cares for the animals, too.
12-20 Praise him for the multi-dimensional Shalom he provides Jerusalem.

Notes
- Praise — Creation/History
- One of the Hallelujah Psalms (146-150).
- One can get the feel of the psalm and a possible clue to its origin by reading of the Dedication of the Wall of Jerusalem: Nehemiah 12:27-43 (especially v. 43).
- The Daily Lectionary suggests this is to be used with the Psalm of the Day, verses 1-11 each Wednesday and verses 12-20 each Thursday.
- "Strengthens the bars of your gates" (v. 13).
- Jerusalem's defenses. (See Nehemiah 4:3, 6, 13-15.)

For Reflection
- See how the psalmist finds delight in meditating upon God's character and all that God has done and continues to do.
- Richardson Wright said, "Proficiency in meditation lies not in thinking much, but in loving much. It is a way of seeking the

divine companionship, the 'closer walk.' Thus it is that meditation has come to be called 'the mother of love.' "

Prayer
Lord God, builder of the heavenly Jerusalem, the city of the living God, we praise you for your power to lift up the downtrodden, to heal the brokenhearted, and to enrich all with your provident care. May we learn to praise you with the love that bears witness of your redeeming grace in Christ toward all that you have made. Amen.

148
Praise The Lord!
Praise The Lord From The Heavens

Praise him, all his angels;
　praise him all his host! ...
Let them praise the name of the Lord,
　for he commanded and they were created ...
Praise the Lord from the earth ...
Mountains and all hills ...
Wild animals and all cattle,
　creeping things and flying birds!
Kings of the earth and all peoples ...
　his glory is above earth and heaven.
　　　　　　　　— Psalm 148:2, 5, 7a, 9a, 10-11a, 13c

Theme: Let all nature praise the Lord

Outline

1-6　Call to heavenly beings and heavenly bodies to praise their Creator.

7-13　Let earth and sea and all their inhabitants (animate and inanimate) praise him.

14　Let Israel — the closest to God — praise him.

Notes
- Praise — Creation/History
- One of the Hallelujah Psalms (146-150).
- "Horn" = a symbol of strength (v. 14).
- Saint Francis based his "Canticle To The Sun" on this psalm. See also a similar canticle, "Song For The Three Children" (inserted after Daniel 3:23 in Roman Catholic Bibles).
- The hymn, "All Creatures Of Our God And King" and other similar hymns take their theme from this psalm.
- The Daily Lectionary suggests this is to be used with the Psalm of the Day each Friday.

For Reflection
- The ancient world looked upon nature as something divine — the gods lurked everywhere. The creation story abolished that idea for the faithful. Our civilization has looked upon nature in terms of conquest and exploitation. The result is becoming a threat to everyone. The psalmist regards nature as a fellow-dependent. We all exist together by God's command.
- A kind of mutual fraternity between man and nature is possible under God. Native Americans sense this, also. We who have degraded nature with our materialist consumerism need urgently to recover a wholesome respect for it.

Prayer

Lord God, what a marvelous universe you have created! What a unique planet you have made. What great artistry you show in it all. Lead us to become good stewards of the earth. May your loving purpose in creation come to glorious fulfillment. May we, together with nature, redeemed from sin and futility, rejoice before you on the great day coming, through Jesus Christ our Lord. Amen.

149
Praise The LORD!
Sing To The LORD A New Song

Let Israel be glad in its Maker,
*   let the children of Zion rejoice in their King ...*
For the LORD takes pleasure in his people;
*   he adorns the humble with victory.*
*   — Psalm 149:2, 4*

Theme: Let Israel praise the Lord

Outline
1-4   Praise the LORD who has restored Israel to dignity and victory.
5-9   Praise him in anticipation of the victorious triumph over all the nations.

Notes
- Praise — Salvation
- One of the Hallelujah Psalms (146-150).
- "New song" is one lived out daily (v. 1). (See Colossians 3:23.) Also the triumphant song in heaven (Revelation 5:9).
- The zealous tone suggests the Maccabbean period, when religious ardor, national enthusiasm, and hatred of national enemies was strong.
- The Daily Lectionary suggests this is to be used with the Psalm of the Day each Saturday.

For Reflection
- This psalm has been misused. It fired up Roman Catholic clergy and laity to undertake the Thirty Years' War. Protestant Thomas Munzer used it to stir up the flames of the Peasants' War.
- While Psalms 2 and 110 tell of the messianic king who will subjugate the nations, this psalm tells of a messianic people who will do it. How?
- Passages such as Matthew 26:52; John 18:36 ("my kingdom is not from this world"); 2 Corinthians 10:3-5 ("the weapons of our warfare are spiritual"); Ephesians 6:17; and Hebrews 4:12

indicate a different interpretation and use of the psalm. The weapon of our warfare is the word of God, the gospel of Christ. The subjugating is the putting down of sin, that the Lord may be king of grace over us and all who believe.

Prayer

Lord God, may all your people rejoice in King Jesus, singing the new song of forgiveness and life through him, and bringing the word of God to people of all nations, that we all may sing the song of the redeemed. Amen.

150
Praise The LORD!
Praise God In His Sanctuary

Let everything that breathes
   praise the LORD!
Praise the LORD!

— Psalm 150:6

Theme: Final jubilant chorus of praise

Notes
- Praise
- One of the Hallelujah Psalms (146-150)

The Psalter, a most marvelous collection of prayers and praises to God ends with this appropriately ecstatic cry of joy. It comes from those who have learned from God not only his great creative power and art, but also his passion for justice and the redeeming of the world, the planet, and its inhabitants. It expresses the joy of knowing that God's elected people are here to bless the world, and their sufferings and sacrificial service are a reflection of the agony in the heart of God, the cost to him of the coming redemption.

The New Testament's doxology in response is:

"You are worthy, our Lord and God,
   to receive glory and honor and power,
for you created all things,
   and by your will they existed and were created."

"You are worthy ...
for you were slaughtered and by your blood you ransomed
      for God
   saints from every tribe and language and people and
      nation;
you have made them to be a kingdom and priests serving our
      God ..."

> *"To the one seated on the throne and to the Lamb*
> *be blessing and honor, and glory and might*
> *forever and ever!"*
> *"Amen!"*
>
> — **Revelation 4:11; 5:9-10, 13b, 14b**

The church of the crucified and risen Lord Jesus Christ responds:

> *We praise you, O God,*
> *we acclaim you as the Lord;*
> *all creation worships you,*
> *the Father everlasting.*
>> *To you all angels, all the powers of heaven,*
>> *the cherubim and seraphim, sing in endless praise:*
>> *Holy, holy, holy Lord, God of power and might,*
>> *heaven and earth are full of your glory.*
>
> *The glorious company of apostles praise you.*
> *The noble fellowship of prophets praise you.*
> *The white-robed army of martyrs praise you.*
> *Throughout the world the holy Church acclaims you:*
>> *Father, of majesty unbounded,*
>> *your true and only Son, worthy of all praise,*
>> *the Holy Spirit, advocate and guide.*
>
> *You, Christ, are the King of glory,*
> *the eternal Son of the Father.*
> *When you took our flesh to set us free*
> *you humbly chose the Virgin's womb.*
>> *You overcame the sting of death*
>> *and opened the kingdom of heaven to all believers.*
>> *You are seated at God's right hand in glory.*
>> *We believe that you will come and be our judge.*
>>> *Come then, Lord, and help your people,*
>>> *bought with the price of your own blood,*
>>> *and bring us with your saints*
>>> *to glory everlasting.*
>
> — **from** *Te Deum Laudamus — A Song of the Church*

Psalm Index

Psalm	Psalm Type	Author/Source	Revised Common Lectionary
Book One			
1	Wisdom Poetry		Easter 7B, Ep 6C
2	Royal Messianic	David	Transfiguration
3	Lament	David	
4	Affirmation of Faith	David	Easter 3B
5	Lament	David	Martyrs
6	Lament — Penitential	David	
7	Lament	David	St. James, Elder
8	Praise — Creation	David	Holy Trinity A, C
9	Acrostic or Alphabetical	David	Communion of Saints
10	Acrostic	David	Pent 16C
11	Affirmation of Faith	David	Sts. Simon and Jude
12	Liturgy	David	St. Bartholomew
13	Lament — Penitential	David	Pent 6A
14	Liturgy — Prophetic	David	Pent 10B, Pent 17C
15	Liturgy — Instruction	David	Ep 4A
16	Affirmation of Faith	David	Easter 2A
17	Lament	David	St. Stephen, Pent 11A
18	Royal Messianic	David	St. Peter
19	Creation and God's word	David	Lent 3B, Pent 17B, Ep 3C, St. Andrew
20	Royal Messianic	David	Pent 4B
21	Royal Messianic	David	
22	Messianic Suffering	David	Good Friday, Lent 2B, Easter 5B, Pent 21B
23	Affirmation of Faith	David	Easter, Baptism, Lent 4A, Easter 4, Burial
24	Liturgy — Instruction	David	All Saints B, Pent 12B, Presentation of our Lord
25	Alphabetical — Meditation	David	Advent 1C, Lent 1B, Confession, Forgiveness
26	Lament	David	Pent 15A, Pent 20A
27	Lament	David	Lent 2C, Ep 3A
28	Lament	David	Lent 5C
29	Creation	David	Epiphany, Holy Trinity B
30	Thanksgiving	David	Easter 3C, Ep 6B, Pent 3A, Pent 6C
31	Lament	David	Easter 5A, Ep 9a, Passion
32	Penitential	David	Lent 1A, Lent 4C
33	Praise — Creation/History		Easter 5A, Pent 12C, Marriage, Prayer at Close of Day

34	Thanksgiving — Alphabetical	David	Pent 12B, Pent 13B, Pent 14B, Pent 23C, All Saint, Baptism, Prayer at Close of Day
35	Imprecatory	David	
36	Mixed	David	Ep 2C, Monday of Holy Week, Confession, Forgiveness
37	Wisdom — Acrostic	David	Ep 7C
38	Penitential	David	
39	Lament	David	
40	Thanksgiving — Lament	David	Ep 2A
41	Thanksgiving — Lament	David	Ep 7B

Book Two

42	Lament	Korahites	Pent 5C, Baptism, Burial
43	Lament		Baptism, Pent 5C
44	National Lament	Korahites	St. Philip, St. James
45	Royal Messianic	Korahites	Pent 7A, Pent 15B, Annunciation, Mary Mother
46	Affirmation of Faith	Korahites	Reformation, Burial
47	Kingship of God/Enthronement	Korahites	Ascension
48	Praise — Zion	Korahites	Pent 7B
49	Wisdom Poetry	Korahites	Pent 11C
50	Liturgy — Prophetic	Asaph	Transfiguration, Pent 12C
51	Penitential	David	Ash Wednesday, Lent 5B – Pent 11B
52	Lament	David	Pent 9C
53	Liturgy — Prophetic	David	
54	Lament	David	Pent 18B
55	Lament — Messianic Suffering	David	
56	Lament — Messianic Suffering	David	St. Matthias
57	Lament	David	St. Mark
58	Lament — Imprecatory	David	
59	Lament	David	
60	Lament	David	
61	Royal Messianic — Lament	David	Pent 3B
62	Affirmation of Faith	David	Ep 3B
63	Lament	David	Lent 3C
64	Lament	David	
65	Praise — Creation/History	David	Pent 23C, Thanksgiving
66	Thanksgiving	David	Easter 6A, Pent 21C

67	Thanksgiving		Easter 6C, Conversion St. Paul
68	Praise — Salvation	David	Easter 7A
69	Imprecatory — Messianic Suffering	David	Pent 3A
70	Lament	David	Wednesday of Holy Week
71	Lament		Ep 4C, Tuesday of Holy Week
72	Royal Messianic	Solomon	Adv 2A, Epiphany

Book Three

73	Wisdom Poetry	Asaph	St. Mary Magdalene
74	Lament	(Asaph)	
75	Thanksgiving	Asaph	
76	Praise	Asaph	
77	Lament	Asaph	
78	History — Salvation	Asaph	Pent 19A, Pent 25A, Pent 6C
79	Lament	(Asaph)	Pent 18C
80	Lament		Adv 4A, Adv 1B, Adv 4C, Pent 13C
81	Liturgy	Asaph	Ep 9B, Pent 2B, Pent 15C
82	Liturgy	Asaph	Pent 8C
83	Liturgy	Asaph	
84	Praise — Zion	Korahites	Presentation, Baptism
85	Liturgy — Prophetic	Korahites	Pent 12A, Adv 2B, Pent 8B, Ep 5C, Peace
86	Lament	David ?	Pent 9A
87	Praise — Zion	Korahite	Sts. Peter and Paul
88	Lament	Korahites	Maundy Thursday
89	Royal Messianic	Ethan	Adv 4B, Pent 9B

Book Four

90	Lament	Moses	Pent 23A, Pent 25A, Burial, Confession, Forgiveness
91	Affirmation of Faith		Lent 1C, Pent 19C, Prayer at Close of Day
92	Thanksgiving		Pent 4B, Ep 8C
93	Kingship of God/Enthronement		Ascension
94	Lament		Renewers of Society
95	Liturgy — Prophetic		Christ the King A, C Lent 3A, Pent 20C
96	Kingship of God/Enthronement		Christmas Eve, Ep 9C
97	Kingship of God/Enthronement		Christmas Day, Easter 7C

98	Kingship of God/Enthronement		Christmas Day, Easter 6B, Pent 25C
99	Kingship of God/Enthronement		Pent 22A, Transfiguration A, Transfiguration C
100	Praise		Pent 4A, Christ the King A, Thanksgiving C, Marriage
101	Royal Messianic		
102	Penitential		New Year's Eve
103	Praise		Ep 8B, St. Michael
104	Praise — Creation		Pentecost, Pent 22B, Stewardship
105	Praise — History		Pent 10A, Pent 12A, Pent 15A, Pent 18A
106	Praise — History		Pent 21A

Book Five

107	Thanksgiving		Pent 11C
108	Mixed — Lament	David?	
109	Imprecatory	David?	
110	Royal Messianic	David?	Ascension
111	Wisdom — Praise		Ep 4B, Pent 13B
112	Wisdom		Ep 5A, Pent 15C
113	Praise		Pent 18C, Visitation
114	Praise — Salvation		Pent 17A
115	Praise — Creation/History		Lent 2B
116	Thanksgiving		Maundy Thursday, Lent 5A, Pent 17B, St. John
117	Praise		Pent 2C, Pent 14C, Marriage
118	Thanksgiving		Palm Sunday, Easter, Easter 2C
119	Acrostic — Alphabetical		Ep 6A, Ep 7A, Pent 8A, Pent 10A, Pent 16A, Pent 24B, Pent 22C, Pent 24C, St. Matthew, Theologians

Pilgrim Songs 120-134 ("Songs of Ascents")

120	Lament		
121	Affirmation of Faith		Lent 2A, Burial
122	Affirmation of Faith		Adv 1A, Baptism
123	Lament		Pent 26A

124	Thanksgiving		Pent 14A, Pent 19B, Holy Innocents, St. Luke
125	Affirmation of Faith		Pent 16B
126	Liturgy		Adv 3B, Lent 5C, Thanksgiving B
127	Wisdom		Pent 25B, Marriage
128	Wisdom		Pent 10A, Marriage
129	Affirmation of Faith		
130	Penitential		Lent 5A, Pent 6B, Pent 12B
131	Affirmation of Faith		Ep 8A
132	Royal Messianic		Christ the King B
133	Liturgy		Pent 13A, Easter 2B, Pent 5B
134	Liturgy		Prayer at Close of Day
135	Praise — Creation/History		Pent 19B
136	Praise — Creation/History		St. Thomas, Marriage, Prayer at Close of Day
137	Lament		Pent 20C
138	Thanksgiving	David	Pent 3B, Ep 5C
139	Wisdom	David	Pent 9A, Ep 2B, Pent 2B, Pent 16C
140	Lament	David	
141	Lament	David	John the Baptist
142	Lament	David	Lent 3A
143	Penitential	David ?	Pent 7B, Burial, Confession, Forgiveness
144	Royal Messianic — Wisdom	David ?	
145	Praise — Acrostic	David ?	Pent 25C
146	Praise — Creation/History		Adv 3A, Pent 24B, Pent 3C
147	Praise — Creation/History		Christmas 2, Ep 5B
148	Praise — Creation/History		Christmas 1, Easter 5C
149	Praise — Salvation		Pent 16A, All Saint C
150	Praise		Easter 2C, Marriage

Psalm types are adapted from *The Layman's Bible Commentary, Psalms*, Vol. 9 by Arnold B. Rhodes, published by John Knox Press.

Liturgical data is from *The Revised Common Lectionary*, published by Augsburg Fortress in 1995.

Lutheran Church Year Psalm Placement

Church Day	Cycle A	Cycle B	Cycle C
Advent 1	122	80	25
Advent 2	72	85	(Luke)
Advent 3	146	126	(Isaiah)
Advent 4	80	89	80
Christmas Eve/Day	96, 97, 98	96, 97, 98	96, 97, 98
Christmas 1	148	148	148
Christmas 2	147	147	147
New Year's (Holy Name)	8	8	8
The Epiphany Of Our Lord	72	72	72
The Baptism Of Our Lord	29	29	29
Epiphany 2	40	139	36
Epiphany 3	27	62	19
Epiphany 4	15	111	71
Epiphany 5	112	147	138
Epiphany 6	119	30	1
Epiphany 7	119	41	37
Epiphany 8	131	103	92
The Transfiguration Of Our Lord	2 or 99	50	99, 97
Ash Wednesday	51	51	51
Lent 1	32	25	91
Lent 2	121	22	27
Lent 3	95	19	63
Lent 4	23	107	32
Lent 5	130	51 or 119	126
Palm Sunday	118	118	118
Sunday Of The Passion	31	31	31
Monday Of Holy Week	36	36	36
Tuesday Of Holy Week	71	71	71
Wednesday Of Holy Week	70	70	70
Maundy Thursday	116	116	116
Good Friday	22	22	22
Holy Saturday	31	31	31
Easter Day	118	118	118
Easter 2	16	133	150
Easter 3	116	4	30
Easter 4	23	23	23
Easter 5	31	22	148
Easter 6	66	98	67
The Ascension Of Our Lord	47 or 93	47 or 93	47 or 93
Easter 7	68	1	97
The Day Of Pentecost	104	104	104
Holy Trinity	8	29	8
Pentecost 2	46 or 31	139 or 81	96

Pentecost 3	33 or 50	138 or 130	146 or 30
Pentecost 4	116 or 100	20 or 92	5 or 32
Pentecost 5	86 or 69	9 or 133	42, 43, or 22
Pentecost 6	13 or 89	130 or 30	77 or 16
Pentecost 7	45 or 145	48 or 123	30 or 66
Pentecost 8	119 or 65	24 or 85	82 or 25
Pentecost 9	139 or 86	89 or 23	52 or 15
Pentecost 10	105 or 119	14 or 145	85 or 138
Pentecost 11	17 or 145	51 or 78	107 or 49
Pentecost 12	105 or 85	130 or 34	50 or 33
Pentecost 13	133 or 67	111 or 34	80 or 82
Pentecost 14	124 or 138	84 or 34	71 or 103
Pentecost 15	105 or 26	45 or 15	81 or 112
Pentecost 16	149 or 119	125 or 146	139 or 1
Pentecost 17	114 or 103	19 or 116	14 or 51
Pentecost 18	105 or 145	1 or 54	79 or 113
Pentecost 19	78 or 25	124 or 19	91 or 146
Pentecost 20	19 or 80	26 or 8	137 or 37
Pentecost 21	106 or 23	22 or 90	66 or 111
Pentecost 22	99 or 96	104 or 91	119 or 121
Pentecost 23	90 or 1	34 or 126	65 or 84
Pentecost 24	107 or 43	146 or 119	119 or 32
All Saints	34	24	149
Pentecost 25	78 or 70	127 or 146	145 or 98
Pentecost 26	123 or 98	16	98
Christ The King	100 or 95	93	46
Thanksgiving Day	65	126	100

Resources

My seminary studies, devotional use of the psalms throughout a long ministry, and a disciplined reading program have been brought to bear on this work. I gratefully acknowledge the following excellent resources:

Luther's Works, Volumes 12, 13, 14, Martin Luther, Concordia Publishing House, St. Louis, 1955.

The Book of Psalms, A. F. Kirkpatrick, Cambridge, Cambridge University Press, 1957.

Psalms, Volumes 1 and 2, George A. F. Knight, *The Daily Study Bible Series*, Westminster Press, Louisville, 1982.

Psalms, The Laymen's Study Bible, Volume 9, Arnold Rhodes, Louisville, John Knox Press 1962.

Reflections On The Psalms, C. S. Lewis, Harcourt, Brace & World, New York, 1958.

Meditations On The Psalms, Dietrich Bonhoeffer, ed. by Edwin Robertson, Zondervan, Grand Rapids, 2002.

Psalms, The Prayer Book of the Bible, Dietrich Bonhoeffer, Augsburg, Minneapolis, 1970.

The Bible Jesus Read, Philip Yancey, Zondervan, Grand Rapids, 2002.

Bede And The Psalter, Benedicta Ward, SLG Press Oxford, England, 1991.

Christ In The Psalms, Patrick Henry Reardon, Conciliar Press, Ben Lomond, California, 2000.

The Psalter, the International Commission on English in the Liturgy, Liturgy Training Publications, Chicago, 1994.

www.ingramcontent.com/pod-product-compliance
Lightning Source LLC
Chambersburg PA
CBHW070934230426
43666CB00011B/2438